9.14.78

QUALITY CONTROLLED INVESTING

QUALITY CONTROLLED
INVESTING

or how to avoid the pick and pray method

FRANK RUSSELL ANDERSON

JOHN WILEY & SONS

New York • Chichester • Brisbane • Toronto

This publication is designed to provide accurate and authoritative information in
regard to the subject matter covered. It is sold with the understanding that the pub-
lisher is not engaged in rendering legal, accounting, or other professional service.
If legal advice or other expert assistance is required, the services of a competent
professional person should be sought. *From a Declaration of Principles jointly
adopted by a Committee of the American Bar Association and a Committee of
Publishers.*

Library of Congress Cataloging in Publication Data:

Anderson, Frank Russell, 1923-
  Quality controlled investing.

  Includes index.
  1. Investments. 2. Stocks. I. Title. II. Title:
How to avoid the pick and pray method.

  HG4521.A59   332.6'78   78-7607
  ISBN 0-471-04382-6

Printed in the United States of America

10 9 8 7 6 5 4 3 2 1

Preface

This book presents for study and adoption a common stock portfolio management system that has its roots in the management-by-objective (MBO) concepts used so successfully by major corporations. The MBO approach tends to be identified as the work of Peter Drucker, whose ideas have been employed extensively throughout the business community. 2025098

Inherent in the premise that MBO concepts can be applied to portfolio management is the thesis that a common stock portfolio constitutes a single business entity. This is in keeping with current interpretations of "prudent man investing" as called for in the 1974 Pension Act (ERISA). It does, however, represent a departure from the conventional view, which sees an assortment of individual issues rather than a business entity.

In order to manage by objectives, it is, of course, necessary to start by setting objectives. Such objectives have to be determined for the entire portfolio, not only for individual issues, and in order to determine appropriate objectives, they must be expressed numerically for the individual issues so that they can be aggregated into total portfolio objectives. The numeric code for the objectives is essential because alphabetic codes can't be employed mathematically.

One valid numerical statement about common stocks and common stock portfolios is *yield*—the percentage relationship between dividend income and market price. Yield serves well as an objective for a management system because it is easily understood, reflects current prices, and can be determined readily, both for the individual issues and for the portfolio as an entity.

The proposal put forth in this book is that investment *quality* can be the second—and balancing—objective needed for an MBO system, using a quality measurement such as the Benchmark® System (a registered trade name issued to the author). The correlation of yield and quality can thus constitute a benchmark by which the suitability of individual issues can be measured. Using such a benchmark, the standard admonition of "buy low, sell high" becomes a very practical strategy.

The benchmark approach to portfolio management is simple, in terms of professional sophistication. And it can be understood and effectively used by investors with no pretense of matching skills with the experts. It is particularly appropriate for the serious investor who wants to make those critical decisions usually reserved for the experts, or at least to have a rational basis for understanding such decisions and, perhaps, challenging them.

Quality Controlled Investing is intended to be a useful book for serious investors, whether they work at it part time or full time. It will probably be more meaningful to investors who use their own money than to money managers who work with other people's funds. Serious investors will likely be found in the executive ranks of corporations and among such professionals as lawyers and doctors. What these people have in common, in addition to a measure of personal wealth, is participation in business management, whether it involves a multi-national corporation or a modest professional firm. All must seek realistic solutions to business problems, usually involving a risk–reward appraisal of a monetary outlay. In such appraisals, the use of bench-marks to clarify the decision-making process is extensive and prob-ably automatic for business executives. It is not possible to evaluate costs and benefits without determining the point that separates "bad" from "good." The quality controlled investment concept applies that form of business problem solving to the management of a common stock investment program. What could be more logical than applying to the investment process the same management system used by the corporations in which one chooses to invest?

But it seems nonsensical to suggest that a part-time investor be pre-pared to spend the time needed to understand a particular company in real depth before investing in it or that participation in the stock market be limited to those who can do so. Even a qualified securities analyst must devote at least 50 hours to such an undertaking, after first spending a year or more in acquiring basic analytical techniques; and even the analyst's capacity is exceeded in attempts to study a complex corporation, many of which now involve dozens of separate businesses.

This is a complex situation, and the response of many prospective investors has been to stay away from the common stock market. The management system that we refer to as *benchmark,* or *quality control, investing* is a practical method that serious investors can use to partici-pate intelligently in the market for common stocks, and its use can serve to rebuild the strength of that market. Further, successful extension of the quality measurement concept, already an integral factor in many industries, to the stock market may spark its use in other consumer markets as well; it is not only prospective investors who are presented with a bewildering variety of choices when they try to make intelligent use of their money but general consumers as well.

FRANK RUSSELL ANDERSON

Chicago, Illinois
February 1978

Contents

QUALITY CONTROLLED INVESTING

CHAPTER ONE

Ideas about Investing

This book presents a logical approach to the buying and selling of common stocks for profit. While the subject has to do with investment strategies and not with business management per se, each investment in common stocks serves to put the investor in partnership with people who, in turn, are making business decisions. It follows that the management system that the investor finds attractive might also be successful if applied to the management of a common stock portfolio.

The management system that has been gaining most rapidly in popularity and effectiveness throughout United States industry is generally identified as management-by-objective, or MBO. All businesses can, of course, claim to be managed according to predetermined objectives, such as making profits. Certainly no one would challenge the validity of such objectives, and their integration into any management system is taken for granted.

The MBO concept does not seek to replace such objectives but, rather, uses them as a starting point. The logic is, granting the premise that objectives do indeed serve to focus business activity toward a specific purpose, that the component activities of a business can be similarly brought to focus by setting individual objectives. Matching and coordinating these component objectives is intended to bring about better overall results for the enterprise. The growing use of the MBO concept strongly suggests that these results are indeed attained.

The apostle of the MBO school of thought, Peter Drucker, repeatedly emphasizes that the goal of a management system is to improve the manager's ability to render judgments. This seems somewhat at odds with our view of a system as a self-contained, self-operating function. The nervous system and the digestive system, for example, function automatically, achieving their objectives without needing to make judgments. Similarly, the solar system proceeds in its own fashion with such predictability that one can aim a rocket at a point in space that, though empty now, will be occupied by a planet when the rocket arrives years hence. Why then must a management system be limited to aiding the formation of judgment?

The answer has to be that the circumstances with which the management system must cope are unpredictable, in sharp contrast to the relationships between physical factors such as weight, energy, and time. If business circumstances were similarly predictable, the manager's role would consist only of turning the system on in the morning and turning it off at night. Instead, the management system has to be content with making it possible for the manager to respond more effectively to varying circumstances by applying better judgment.

The successes of the MBO concept during the past few decades need not be detailed here, but they have been impressive. Not all of the systems have been equally effective; but the purchaser of IBM common stock, for example, benefits from one of the more sophisticated and successful MBO systems.

The market for common stocks is also characterized by unpredictability, and we find that fruitful parallels can be drawn between the sense of how to succeed in business versus the sense of how to meet the profit objectives of buying and selling common stocks. In particular, we see that the common element that motivates the business community as well as those who enter the stock market has to do with the central role played by investment in these two domains.

To start a business involves investment. Usually physical space will be needed, capital items purchased, and salaries of managers and workers paid. Inventories may be needed, and a reserve of operating funds to sustain solvency as the business pump is being primed is necessary. The investment monies may come from external sources, such as unsecured or secured loans or the sales of common stock. In time, the business profits provide an internal source of funds for investing. Not only does a business start with investment but it also has recurring investments. And reinvestments, like gasoline for the internal combustion engine, are the fuel that keeps a business going.

Business managers almost invariably base investment decisions on the need for generating future income. But, because risks are always involved to one degree or another, decision-makers must compare the anticipated rewards against a rational estimate of the risks. Decisions about whether this equipment should be purchased, or this new product developed, or this new marketing program launched are representative of those that continuously confront the business people who rely on the MBO system to improve their judgments.

The market where common stocks are bought and sold is also where investment-minded people are found. And even though some people have become rich and others poor, the point of investing in this market has the same goal as any business venture—to make a profit and avoid a loss. The aim of this book, then, is to describe a way for investors to function effectively and rationally in the common stock market.

No system can remove all the risk for investors who want to show a profit from their activity, whether directly in business or in the securities markets. Even sniffing and pinching cheese can only give an indication, not a definite proof, that one item should be purchased rather than another. On the other hand, it is never a disadvantage to buy and sell when one has reliable information about the product.

It is clear that investors of all types are seeking a suitable reward for giving up temporary control of their money. Most realize that risks are involved and therefore the aim is to balance the rewards against the risks; that is, to "optimize" the situation. To risk the loss of a dollar for the chance to win a dollar by the flip of a "fair" coin, however, is neither a good nor a bad investment, even though no sensible person will play this so-called zero-sum game with any less favorable odds.

But investors in the real world, whether business managers or stock purchasers, can never know exactly what the odds on the success of a particular venture will be. Because of these inherent uncertainties, the investor or manager is left to estimate the probabilities on the basis of what actually is known. If a judgment is reached that the rewards seem to justify the risks, then the investment will be made. The ability to render good judgments is therefore critical to success.

Decision theory is the mode for reaching rational judgments about which investments make the most sense. And when the odds clearly favor a particular investment, no one should complain when an occasional loss is suffered. To flip a fair coin and risk the loss of one dollar for the chance to gain two is a good deal even if occasionally a dollar is lost. This is so because, in the long term, after many flips of the coin, a respectable profit will be realized.

To some extent, stock market investing may be regarded as making an investment judgment that is, in turn, based on the business judgment of a corporation. The concurrence between the profit motives of the investor and those of the corporation in which he or she invests is, of course, an advantage. But hard decisions have to be made at several levels to achieve a mutually favorable outcome.

According to the axioms of decision theory, investments optimally are made when based on all of the known information. Also, a weighting should be involved to take into account the relative quality of the available information. For example, to know that a company has been in a growth mode during the last several years is important information to the stock market investor, but not as important as the information (if true) that the company is on the verge of losing its key managers.

In the final analysis, investment decisions are made in expectation of an income stream as measured in terms of reliability and size. That is, a "good" investment is taken to be one that produces sizable and certain profits over a considerable period of time—a long enough period to assure recovery of the investment plus some additional years of profit. Thus, in business, if the nature of the project is such that as many as 10 years will be required to recover the investment, then a high degree of reliability will be wanted for the income stream. With a shorter recovery period, lesser reliability may be tolerated.

What we are describing here as a "good" investment can also be referred to as an investment of *high quality*. This way of speaking— and thinking—takes on special meaning as soon as rational ways are found to define and to measure quality. In other words, when an investor can say how good, good is, then he or she has a basis for making (or not making) investments with added confidence about the eventual outcome.

Decision-making processes comparable to those that are a feature of good business practices are also encountered and employed by investors in the market for bonds and preferred stocks. In Chapter 2 we will see how the reliability of the income stream for these securities is logically measured and expressed in terms of quality ratings. When suitably chosen quality factors can be of critical importance in the allocation of investible funds, investors are consistently willing to pay a higher price for high quality. The predictable result is that the market for the senior securities tends to be orderly (logical) and relatively safe.

As we have noted, investment in common stocks puts money to work for people who need financing for their business decisions. Remarkably, however, the investment community generally assumes that investing in common stocks involves an approach that is more mysterious and magical (and hence less rational) than the businesslike decisions that are employed in the markets for senior securities and in the allocation of investible funds within a successful business.

Historically myths have tended to emerge in the merchandising of common stocks that imply that such investments are not susceptible to an intelligent approach for employing capital. As a result, the market for common stocks has characteristically been chaotic and fundamentally irrational, in distinct contrast to the stable behavior of the bond and preferred stock markets.

Here we take the position that successful investing in common stocks should involve the same kind of rational and intelligent decision-making that goes into the operation of any other sound business activity. Since the MBO concept has proven to be successful in so many activities, we suggest that it should be applied as well in the management of a common stock portfolio.

As we noted earlier, the benchmarks used by business managers in distinguishing between good and bad investments are the amount of income to be generated (return on investment) and the reliability, or certainty, that such income will in fact be forthcoming. The equivalent factors in the investor's language are referred to as *yield* and *investment quality*—the latter being defined as a *proven* ability to earn profits and pay dividends.

The information available to the investor in these two areas is far superior to the information on which a business manager must rely. The exact amount of a business investment is rarely known at decision-making time—cost overruns are common in business—but the cost of acquiring 100 shares of common stock can be determined quickly and accurately. Forecasting the income to be derived from a business investment almost always represents a leap into the unknown, which is justified by subjective interpretation of possibly relevant data. By contrast, dividend payments are a matter of historical record and can be predicted with great accuracy for most common stocks.

Considering the superiority of the information available to investors, an MBO system should prove to be even more effective in the common stock market than it has in business.

The key to successful investing, in our view, is to employ objective quality ratings for common stocks in combination with the income stream, or yield, as management objectives in a portfolio management system. In this way, we provide a logical means for investors to employ rational strategies as they enter the common stock market, comparable to those enjoyed by investors in the bond and preferred stock markets.

Quality ratings can serve the rational investor by exposing the market's excesses. Such excesses, when not justified in terms of quality, will signal a buying opportunity or a selling opportunity. The system therefore will do what it is supposed to do—improve the manager's ability to make judgments.

The essential structure of this management system can be seen in Figure 1.1. An objective is set for the portfolio in terms of a coordinate point reflecting a quality index and a yield. In this instance, the objectives are a quality index of 6500 and a yield of 4%, and these are marked on the chart with a tolerance of plus or minus 10%. The horizontal line drawn through the target zone represents the range dur-

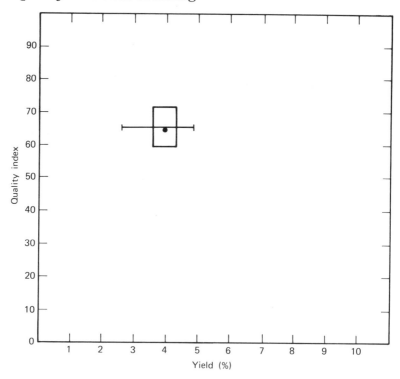

Figure 1-1. Essential structure of common stock investment management system (range of yield on the common stock of Continental Oil Company, 1975).

ing 1975 of the yield on the common stock of Continental Oil Company, an issue meeting the assigned quality level.

Figure 1.1 illustrates that Continental Oil common is suitable for the portfolio when, based on the current price, it yields more than 4.4% and therefore appears to the right of the target area. In order to traverse the target area, the price must rise at least 22%, at which time the system signals a selling opportunity. If the price declines and the yield increases, assuming no change in quality, the system signals a buying opportunity.

Since it is scarcely practical or desirable to invest in a single common stock, most portfolios will involve the blending of numerous stocks, some of high quality, some of low quality. The most truthful statement ever made about the stock market is that attributed to J. P. Morgan who has been quoted as saying, "It will fluctuate." As prices fluctuate, yields change, and the position of individual stocks on the chart will also change. Nonetheless, the management system holds these fluctuations in perspective, relative to the portfolio objectives, and thereby enables the manager (or investor) to make effective judgments.

The chaotic character of the stock market is ample evidence that managers (or investors) have been pursuing inappropriate objectives and making poor judgments. Generally, the investor congratulates himself if a stock that sold at 20 on Monday sells at 22 on Friday. The difference in market price, however, is not an achievement unless the investor actually bought on Monday and sold on Friday. Rather, it is a change in circumstances to which the investor must respond. The wholesale retreat from the stock market by individual investors, best exemplified by the withdrawal of assets from mutual fund managers, strongly suggests a growing conviction that such responses and judgments have been inadequate. The time is therefore particularly appropriate to explore the concept of quality-oriented, systematic management for common stock portfolios.

CHAPTER TWO

Present Applications for Investment Quality

The measurement of investment quality for senior securities, such as bonds and preferred stocks, is an established practice. These measurements are updated and published from time to time so that buyers and sellers can meet their objectives with added certainty. Less advanced is the use of investment quality measurement for common stocks; this book is aimed at correcting that situation.

Investment quality is a widely used but rarely defined term that, when applied to common stocks, means the proven ability to earn profits and pay dividends. Obviously, if an objective and comparable system for measuring common stock investment quality were brought into active use, it would supply a vital additional dimension for portfolio management. The reason: there would be a pragmatic basis for replacing intuitive management with systematic management.

The most familiar form of quality measurements are the bond ratings published by Moody's Investors Service and by Standard & Poor's Corporation, which have been in extensive use for decades. It is virtually impossible to sell bonds in large amounts without first obtaining a rating by one or both of these agencies.

The measurement of bond quality has thus become an integral part of the functioning of the bond markets. In consequence, quality ratings are the predominant factor in determining the fair price to be paid for bonds. Higher quality issues command the higher price.

Another reflection of the validity of these current measures of bond quality is seen in the inverse relationship between quality and investment yield per annum—that is, the ratio of the current income to

TABLE 2.1 MOODY BOND RATINGS AND ASSOCIATED YIELDS

Rating	Yield (%)	Yield Index
Aaa	9.14	100
Aa	9.78	107
A	10.14	111
Baa	10.93	112

the purchase price. An example of actual Moody ratings and the associated yields as of a given date are shown in Table 2.1. Yields associated with Moody ratings, of course, vary from time to time; but the pattern of lower yields correlating with the higher quality issues is consistent as well as logical. By and large, bond investors are prepared to accept a lower yield when their objective is to maximize the certainty of bond redemption at maturity.

In the Moody system the Baa bonds are referred to as *medium grade*. The A bonds are taken to be of somewhat better quality and, in Table 2.1, are seen to yield about 8% less $[= (10.93 - 10.14)/ 10.93]$ to the owner. The Aa bonds are of still higher quality, therefore presenting a still lower yield. And the Aaa bonds represent the best grade available, and therefore the lowest yield. This actual tabulation clearly demonstrates the close inverse correlation between quality and yield. It shows that the bond market recognizes investment quality (as defined and measured by Moody in the present case) and is willing to pay for it.

To illustrate this willingness, yield index numbers are shown in the third column of Table 2.1. Yield indices are formed by dividing the yield associated with each rating by the yield associated with the top Aaa rating. Hence, the yield index of the top rating provides a reference index of 100.

Now, comparing the yield index data, the conclusion can be drawn that on the particular date to which the tabulated data refer, the market was making essentially no distinction between the lowest (Baa) and the next lowest (A) ratings. On the other hand, it is clear that on the reference date more credence was being given to the quality difference between the lower and the upper grades. That the top (Aaa) grade was more highly regarded than the neighboring (Aa) grade also is clear.

Although the correlation between yield (and yield index) with quality is strong, it is the way the differentials (that reflect the correlation) change from time to time that has special diagnostic value. For example, the figures presented in Table 2.1 refer to market conditions during a severe recession—the data indicate a buyer preference for quality, that is, for the preservation of capital.

In periods of greater prosperity and optimism, the quality rating versus yield data tends to reflect a willingness on the part of buyers to accept higher yields along with greater risks by favoring the lower quality issues. Their aim in such instances might be, for example, to achieve an overall blending of high and low quality issues in a portfolio that is being focused on a particular yield objective.

It should be understood that the currently used systems for measuring the investment quality of bond issues provide *comparative* ratings but not quantified ones. No attempt is made to suggest that numerical values can be given to the various categories, much less to the differences between them. In effect, all the systems say is that the Aaa bonds are "better" than the lower quality Aa bonds.

Thus, in the example given in Table 2.1, the Aaa issues are better than the Aa issues, and the A issues are better than the Baa issues. However, there is no implication that these differences can be reduced to a set of numbers. Nor should it be thought that this lack of quantitative differentiation constitutes a fault or shortcoming of the investment measurement systems for bond quality ratings. On the contrary, the widespread use and acceptance by investors and security analysts of these systems confirm that they serve a useful, perhaps indispensable, purpose.

In fact, the use of alphabetical expressions for quality rating conveniently guards against misunderstandings of the sort under discussion. Obviously, if the Baa bonds had been given the numeric designation 1, and the Aaa bonds the designation 4, the tendency might be to conclude that Aaa issues are four times as good as the Baa issues. It is not the purpose of current systems to provide such judgments.

What, then, is the sense of a measure of the investment quality of corporate bonds? Clearly, the relationship between historical corporate earnings and the cost of servicing the incurred debt will be an important factor. Implicit in this idea is the presumption that the future can be predicted by analysis of past events. Of course, probabilities have to be taken into consideration, but bond ratings continue to be widely used without explicit reference to the theory of probability and were developed before probability theory was extensively known. It can be argued that bond ratings gave de facto recognition to probability theory before the latter was widely used.

In any case, the most important calculation to be made for the measurement of bond quality rating is the ratio of earnings available for paying interest to actual interest charges. Naturally, a company that earns its interest liabilities 10 times a year can claim bond issues of higher quality than another company whose earnings cover the annual interest charges only 5 times annually.

The ratio of net income to principal payments also constitutes another important factor for comparison. And although other factors may logically also be considered, the basic thrust of viable systems must always be to sensibly measure the company's ability to earn enough money to cover the ongoing and recurring interest and principal requirements.

Quality measurement for preferred stock similarly is an accepted and useful practice. The ratings are not as widely known because there are fewer preferred stocks than bonds, and the former is a less active market than the latter. Even so, investment quality measures for preferred stocks do play an influential role in the market.

Some sample ratings, yields, and yield indices are shown in Table 2.2, as taken from a representative Standard & Poor's publication. The implied range of quality is from medium grade (BBB) to top grade (AAA). Again, the correlation between quality and yield is apparent; however, the overall range in yield (and yield index) is much wider. Indices ranging from 100 to 153 for preferred stocks are thus to be compared with those ranging from 100 to 112 for bonds. The interpretation of this disparity illuminates why quality rating methods are so useful. For example, in assessing the probability that particular

TABLE 2.2 STANDARD & POOR'S PREFERRED
STOCK RATINGS AND ASSOCIATED YIELDS

Rating	Yield (%)	Yield Index
AAA	7.75	100
AA	8.70	112
A	10.68	137
BBB	11.93	153

bond issues will meet their interest payment obligations, the measurement system has only to determine the probability that the interest will be earned. If it is earned, then it must be paid; hence, no other uncertainties need be considered.

To assess the probability that the dividends of preferred stocks will be paid, however, involves the weighing of several factors:

1. *Will the bond interest be earned and paid?* Because interest has a prior claim on earnings, dividends on the preferred stock can't be considered until the interest charges have been met.
2. *Will the cash flow be sufficient to pay off scheduled amounts of debts?* The debt service also has a prior claim over preferred dividends, and must be given priority by the corporate directors.
3. *Will there be earnings sufficient to pay a preferred stock dividend?* An affirmative answer, of course, means that both the bond interest and associated debt have first been paid and that profits still remain in an amount at least equal to the dividend.
4. *Will the directors, in fact, declare a dividend?* Payment of every preferred stock dividend requires a positive action on the part of the board of directors. Because payments can be deferred at the option of the directors, it is necessary to assess the probability of that happening.

Indeed, all those questions refer to what may or may not be happening at some later time. It's just like buying Grade A eggs in the supermarket. You are betting on (and paying a premium price for) the likelihood that chickens won't be hatching in the immediate future. As with bond quality ratings, implicit in the measurement of the investment quality of preferred stocks is the idea that past history is a valid predictor of future events.

The wide acceptance by investors of the quality system for preferred stocks provides sufficient affirmation that comparisons based on it have value. Again, and as in the case of the bond ratings, alphabetical rather than numeric terms are used to express quality. This means that one can say with confidence that the AAA preferred stocks are higher in quality than the AA issues. The degree of difference, in relative as well as absolute terms, is, however, left unspecified.

To summarize, we have indicated that quality measurements have demonstrated value for investors in the senior securities markets. It is true that the preferred stock ratings tend to be less definitive than those for bond issues, but quality ratings have high acceptance in both markets. The fact that higher quality issues sell at lower yield is all the proof that is needed to demonstrate that use of quality ratings has become influential in investment decision-making.

We now look at the question of whether it makes sense to develop quality rating measures for common stocks. Standard & Poor's Corporation does, in fact, publish common stock rankings, identified by such symbols as A+, A, A—, and B+, but refers to them as *scorings*. Despite the similarities in the codes (Aaa to Baa for bonds, AAA to BBB for preferred stocks, and A+ to B+ for common stocks), present common stocks rating systems represent a drastic departure from the concepts employed for rating bonds and preferred stocks. The cited common stock scorings result from assessments of many factors, including the company's size, industry position, financial policy, and managerial capability. Such factors, unfortunately, involve the application of generally subjective judgments. And this is far different from the objective measurement of the "number of times per annum that interest is earned" that dominates the bond rating system. Standard & Poor's goes so far as to emphasize that their common stock ratings should *not* be confused with the investment quality ratings for bonds. It is to be expected, therefore, that the correlation between quality and yield seen for the senior securities will not be evident in the case of common stock issues.

To test this conclusion, 20 common stock issues were selected at random in the Standard & Poor's top four categories (5 in each category) so that the comparison between scoring and yield could be observed. The result of the data analysis is shown in Table 2.3. A study of the sampling shows that, although the market tends to accept the top (A+) rating and is willing to accept the associated lower yields, the quality/yield correlation in the other categories is weak. The con-

TABLE 2.3 STANDARD & POOR'S COMMON STOCK SCORING OF 20 RANDOM ISSUES AND ASSOCIATED YIELDS

Scoring	Yield					Average (%)
A+	2.21%	2.14%	1.90%	3.76%	1.71%	2.34
A	5.60	1.82	8.99	6.69	4.88	5.61
A	5.69	1.05	3.35	5.43	5.77	4.32
B+	3.61	8.69	2.89	3.56	3.81	4.51

clusion, therefore, is that the Standard & Poor's rating system for common stocks is not fulfilling the role of facilitating decision-making as is the case of the investment quality ratings for bonds and preferred stocks.

There are, of course, considerations other than yield that influence a market for common stocks. Stock selections for a portfolio should be concerned with what might be termed the "appropriateness" of the stock rather than with a yield/quality relationship alone. Appropriateness is a function of the investor's objective, which is narrowly defined for a bond portfolio but not for common stocks. One objective might be capital appreciation, another might be income or anything else.

Still, the point is that objectives are known only to the investor. That is, an investor may have a variety of reasons, other than yield, for buying a stock. These reasons are privately held and, therefore, do not directly influence the balance of the market. As a result, the demand for individual stocks will ebb and flow over time, for reasons that are obscure and often unconnected with usual investment factors.

Obviously, what is wanted is a rating system for common stocks that will assist the private investor to react profitably to those changes in demand even though the causes are unknown. This is the subject we discuss in the following chapters of this book (particularly in Chapters 4, 5, 6, and 7).

For now we return to Table 2.3 because it reveals some of the vagaries that are commonplace in the stock market. For example:

1. There is a wide range between the high and low yields associated with the stock issues in each category. Thus, in the two middle groups (A and A−) the range is more than four to one, while in the top and median groups (A+ and B+) the range is about three to one.

2. In the three categories below top quality, there is an obvious abberation: a stock (or stocks) with yields lower than the average of those in the next higher quality category.

The demand for common stocks, characteristically, will be more-or-less unpredictable at any specific point in time. And this is why it seems unlikely that a definition of investment quality can be found that shows a strong correlation between quality and yield. The complexity of anticipating the demand for these stocks poses too much of a problem.

It does seem likely, however, that the quality of common stocks can be defined in an objective and comparative way, such that the resultant quality and yield data will provide useful "benchmarks" against which the demand for a stock can be tested. To the extent that this is true, common stock quality measurements can become the base of a new and rational approach to the management of portfolios according to each investor's objectives. Specifically, the aim would be to disclose otherwise hidden buying and selling opportunities.

To be effective, however, the wanted quality measurement system should match the specifications of those other systems by which the quality of bonds and preferred stocks now are adduced. In particular, it must be objective and comparative because these are the features that underlie the acceptance and utility of the senior securities systems we described above.

As we stated at the beginning of this chapter, investment quality, when applied to common stocks, should be a valid measure of the proven ability of each issuer to earn profits and pay dividends. The definition seems simple enough, but until now there has been a reluctance to recognize the application possibility. For one thing, there has been the physical problem of accumulating and comparing the available data necessary to develop an objective and comparative system. With the advent of the high-speed computer, this obstacle has been reduced. Indeed, that is why it has been possible to write this book now.

As we shall see in the next chapter, the Benchmark System of measuring investment quality for common stocks is essentially based on a statistical analysis of available data gathered over a 10-year period. Such analysis, however, differs greatly from the traditional investment analysis employed in investment decision making. Hence, the reader is cautioned against confusing the two types of analyses. The statistical analysis we are talking about is aimed at showing each company's ability to solve their management problems successfully over a period of time. Statistical analyses are indeed essential as the strong tendency toward corporate conglomerating makes it increasingly difficult for even a professional analyst to understand much more about a corporation than its proven ability to earn profits and pay dividends.

It is, however, important to add that although sophisticated computer processing of complicated statistical data is involved in the Benchmark computation of common stock investment quality ratings, the use of these ratings is simple and straightforward. In other words, private investors without special training or computer access can use the Benchmark ratings as a personal guide to portfolio management.

A truism of the investment fraternity is that a good stock is one that goes up. However, the statement seems to suggest also that a stock that does not go up is a bad stock. This is far from true, and a quality measurement system can be an effective tool in exposing buying (and selling) opportunities created by obscure market trends. Limiting its scope to this specific purpose eliminates the need for the system to evaluate the full spectrum of concerns that enter into a buy or sell decision.

Measuring Common Stock Investment Quality

"When you can measure what you are speaking about and express it in numbers, you know something about it; but when you cannot measure it, when you cannot express it in numbers, your knowledge is of a meagre and unsatisfactory kind." This was the perceptive comment of a great British physicist, Lord Kelvin, in 1891. The use of numerical investment quality measurements is proposed in this book so that investors can trade in the stock market without relying solely on knowledge "of a meagre and unsatisfactory kind."

It is sometimes argued, of course, that knowledge about common stock investing differs fundamentally from knowledge about physical things. Economics is often spoken of as a "soft" science to distinguish it from the "hard" sciences such as physics. What this view overlooks is that, in Kelvin's time, the importance of precise measurements was just evolving; agreement on the measurement system in itself helped make the hard sciences more exact and predictable. If the state of economic theory is lagging behind that of physics today, the development and refinement of feasible measurements, such as the investment quality of common stocks, surely constitutes a step in the right direction.

The introduction of quality measurement into American business apparently occurred late in the nineteenth century with the "good, better, best," code of quality used by Sears, Roebuck & Company in its mail order activities. Although simple in nature, the code clearly expressed a differential in quality categories. The success of this concept is reflected in its continuing to be an essential part of Sears' very successful merchandising effort.

The interesting question that arises is concerned with the value that Sears saw in this quality code. An obvious alternative to using a quality measurement would be to offer a single category of goods. A liberal merchandise return policy and a reliable retailer would seem to be simpler, and less inexpensive, than introducing the complexities of product quality. Why, then, would Sears add this complicating factor to its merchandising system?

The answer has to lie in the impact of the price differential on the size of the market. Sears must have been convinced that customers would recognize and appreciate differentials in quality and would therefore be willing to pay different prices for different levels of quality. Accepting this premise, the introduction of quality measurements broadened the available market because potential buyers would no longer be limited to the group that was satisfied with a good *or* a better *or* a best product.

Another move toward quality measurement of consumer products was the introduction in 1906 of meat inspection by the United States Department of Agriculture (USDA). In its early stages, this measurement system was basically one of distinguishing between good and bad meat processing, with the latter seriously threatening the health of the public. During the 1920s, however, a comprehensive grading system was started, rating meat as *prime, choice, commercial,* or *cutter* quality.

It is of considerable interest that the meat quality measurement program, although actually conducted by the USDA, was initially fostered by the major meat packers and continues to be a voluntary program which is paid for by the processors themselves. Thus the measurement system was not imposed by government action on the industry but, rather, was sought by the processors, presumably in order to improve their ability to do business.

Poultry products are also graded by the USDA into three quality categories—A, B, and C. The principle criterion seems to be appearance, and retailers rarely distribute anything but Grade A products. Nonetheless, the industry must feel that this measurement system is economically valid, since it, too, is both voluntary and paid for by the processors.

Another category of product which the USDA measures for quality is butter. Here again there are three quality categories—AA, A, and B. The differential between the two top categories is fairly modest but is reflected consistently in a price differential. The Grade B product is significantly lower in quality and sells at a significantly lower price.

There are two observations that can be drawn from the continued use of these measurement systems. First, industry finds quality measurement to be of value to the point that businesses enter into the activity voluntarily and also pay its entire cost. Second, there is consistently a relationship between quality levels and the price of the products.

One of the observations made about the market for common stocks, which is intended to distinguish it from the market for tangible products, is that stocks relate to intangible values. Because of this single concern, it is sometimes argued that practices appropriate to these other markets are not functional or rational for the common stock market.

In point of fact, the measurement of at least one intangible was well developed before the USDA quality measurement systems were established in the 1920s—human intelligence, which began to be measured by Alfred Binet in France during the years 1905–1911. Stanford University conducted additional research, and as early as 1915 revised the original Binet test. A book published in 1916, called *The Measurement of Intelligence,* made the Stanford-Binet testing process an integral part of American society and education.

The introduction of intelligence measurement had a profound impact on American society. Many states enacted so-called sterilization laws as early as 1907 in the belief that inferior intelligence was hereditary and should be weeded out. Extensive IQ testing of draftees during World War I provided a data base that was employed extensively in determining immigration policies by the Congress during the 1920s. The continued use of this basic system, although it has been modified as a result of experience, is ample evidence indeed that intangible values can be not only measured but also widely accepted and useful.

An interesting result of the introduction of IQ measurement was its effect in moving genius, or high intelligence, out of the area of mysticism and magic. Historically, genius was identifiable only by the acts of gifted individuals who often used these unmeasured powers to enhance their political and social positions. These became the oracles and witch doctors who employed their intelligence in a functional manner to baffle their communities.

If an intangible like intelligence can be measured numerically, there should be no reason why investment quality cannot also be measured, and, in fact, it is. Quality measurements of bonds and preferred stocks, as we have said, are widely accepted by investing professionals. However, quality measurements of common stocks are not widely available.

A principal drawback of current investment quality measurements is that the ratings are alphabetic, not numeric. Following the dictum of Lord Kelvin, the utility of any measurement system is greatly enhanced as soon as a logical basis can be found to have quality expressed on a numerical scale in order to facilitate comparisons. Because currently used quality ratings of securities are not numerical, they can be applied to individual issues but cannot be used to generate statistical statements about total portfolios. And so-called portfolio management consists essentially of selecting individual issues, because there is no arithmetic means for coordinating such selections with an overall portfolio objective.

In contrast to this "pick-and-pray" approach, prudent management dictates that the portfolio be regarded as a single business entity; this, too, is impossible when using alphabetical quality codes. Quality control can be achieved only by setting a standard for the entire portfolio and directing the manager to maintain it. Unless such a standard can be calculated, the management directive boils down to "do the best you can."

The selection of a quality standard is greatly facilitated by a universal numerical code because comparison is thus made possible. Every portfolio need not have the same standard, and nonprofessional investors in particular may find it difficult to select one. If, however, they could compare Prudential's "Piece of the Rock" option with a mutual fund or some individual portfolios, they would have a frame of reference for setting their own objectives.

Another drawback of the alphabetic systems is that they employ few quality categories, usually no more than six or seven. When introduced, these were probably adequate. Now, however, there are at least 4100 actively traded common stocks, meaning that each such category must include hundreds of companies. The resulting wide range of quality tends to make the categorization of little value.

The determination of portfolio quality using numerical measurements is, in mathematical terms, extremely simple and consists basically of calculating a weighted average of the quality ratings of the component holdings. Each holding is weighted according to its market value and quality factor so that totals for both weighted and unweighted values can be determined. The weighted aggregate value is then divided by the unweighted total to provide the quality index. Such a calculation is simple to perform, even by hand; modern calculators and computers make it possible to calculate and compare portfolio quality quickly and cheaply.

Although quality measurement of common stocks is not as extensively used as it is for bonds and preferred stocks, there are a number of systems presently in use. Major investing institutions make quality measurements of common stocks but generally retain them for their exclusive in-house use.

In the absence of a universal measurement system, the author developed the Benchmark System for measuring the investment quality of common stocks. This is a statistical system that operates by computer and thus meets the standards of objectivity and universal applicability. The Benchmark ratings are expressed in a numerical code ranging from 1 to 99.

In the Benchmark System, a large number of companies are compared, over a 10-year period, on their ability to earn profits and pay dividends. Each is then compared against all of the others and ranked on the basis of these criteria. After the ranking is completed, the total group of about 3000 companies is divided into percentiles, and the percentiles are used as the numerical quality index. Thus each quality category covers approximately 30 issues, not several hundred.

That quality measurements of common stock portfolios are made as a matter of course by institutions and money managers is interesting for several reasons. First, it supports the premise that investment quality is indeed measurable. Such a premise is sustained by careful consideration of the term "investment quality" and what it means. A proven ability to earn profits and pay dividends, the accepted definition of common stock quality, clearly involves historical facts that are ascertainable from the financial records. Incorporating those facts into a measurement system thus becomes a statistical exercise, one that is readily accomplished with modern computing devices.

Second, the existence of private measurement systems indicates recognition on the part of the industry that investment quality must be important. It seems to be an accepted fact of life that data processing managers never have—in their eyes—an adequate budget; those in investing institutions are no exceptions. Thus the allocation of some portion of that precious budget to quality measurement must be based on the recognition that it is a worthwhile activity.

A similar line of reasoning leads to the conclusion that quality measurement must also be relatively cheap—or at least not exorbitantly expensive. If the activity involved a major expenditure, it surely would be widely advertised and probably offered for sale. That the measurements are reserved largely for internal use, or made available only to selected customers, suggests strongly that cost is not a serious problem. The author's experience with the Benchmark System supports this conclusion.

It can also be logically deduced that there is general agreement on the definition of investment quality among these institutions and their customers. Little purpose would be served by producing a measurement that had to be redefined and explained every time it was employed.

Agreement on the definition, however, does not necessarily mean universal agreement on the operations of the system. Each developer selects those criteria he believes will be most useful in achieving the designated objective and processes them in his own way. Thus, the Benchmark System uses a 10-year history—another system might use 5 years, still another might prefer 12.

The major disadvantage of existing measurement systems is their lack of universality and interchangeability. Each institution cherishes its system as unique and superior; little credibility is given to others. The discrepancies occur largely in the number of quality categories used and the amount of subjective interpretation. Few systems involve more than a dozen quality categories and none approaches the 99 used in the Benchmark System.

Some concrete examples of the techniques that can be used in developing investment quality measurement systems can be noted to support the assertion that this is indeed a practical activity. To begin with the simplest, it is arguable that the essence of investment quality can be expressed in a single ratio. The definition "an ability to earn profits and pay dividends" can be paraphrased to read "an ability to use the resources available to management so as to pay dividends to the owners." Statistically, that property can be expressed by determining the ratio between dividends paid and stockholders' equity. The presumption is that dividends will be distributed to the maximum extent consistent with the needs of the business and that the resources available to management consist of the owners' equity. For illustration, we use the record of Quaker Oats Company shown in Table 3.1; note that the time span is 10 years. The series of ratios shown in Table 3.1, in order to be useful for ranking purposes, must be reduced to a single number. One approach might be to calculate the growth rate evidenced by the ratio, which, in the Quaker Oats case, would be negative. An average for the period could be determined, as could a median, or the ratios could simply be aggregated. The test would be considered valid, given the initial premise, so long as it was applied identically to all of the companies tested.

Although the single-ratio approach is arithmetically feasible, it is inadequate in terms of investment statistics. A more comprehensive formula, using three ratios, produces ranking numbers for Quaker and

TABLE 3.1   RATIO BETWEEN DIVIDENDS PAID AND OWNERS' EQUITY,
QUAKER OATS COMPANY

(*in millions of dollars*)

Year	Dividends	Equity	Ratio (%)
1	10.1	169.2	5.97
2	11.0	184.6	5.96
3	12.0	197.2	6.09
4	13.0	217.7	5.97
5	13.9	232.0	5.99
6	14.1	259.6	5.43
7	14.9	312.8	4.76
8	15.7	338.4	4.64
9	16.6	400.7	4.14
10	17.4	431.8	4.03

four other midwestern companies, as shown in Table 3.2. It should be
noted that these data are samples only, taken from test runs by the
computer, and no conclusions should be drawn from them.

It is again apparent from Table 3.2 that companies can be
ranked on the basis of selected ratios. The principal deficiencies in
this approach are, first, that the number of tests is inadequate and, second, that there is no weighting of the results. In using a time series of

TABLE 3.2   SAMPLE RANKINGS OF FIVE MIDWESTERN
COMPANIES

Company	Ranking	Percentile
Stewart-Warner	3723.430	79
Quaker Oats	3579.840	73
Sears Roebuck	3431.430	68
Jewel Companies	3361.980	64
Marshall Field	3357.810	64

investment data, more recent results are more significant and should be given greater weight than results from earlier years. Similarly, the accumulation of numerous ratios must be done in such a manner as to give proper weight to each test.

The weighting process can produce significantly different results for the same five companies, as indicated in Table 3.3. It should be noted that the magnitude of the ranking number has no significance in itself. For ranking purposes, the computer doesn't care whether there are five digits to the left of the decimal or seven digits to the right.

These illustrations demonstrate clearly that a measurement system can indeed be constructed for determining the investment quality of common stocks. The process is probably not practical without a computer, in view of the numerous necessary calculations, but the logic for the system can be seen in these samples.

In addition to calculating quality at a given point in time, the yearly calculations form a quality profile showing how, over the 10-year span, the quality rating was built up. This can be shown graphically by charting the individual years, as shown in Figure 3.1, again using Quaker Oats data for illustration. No particular conclusion should be drawn from Figure 3.1, as the purpose here is simply to illustrate a statistical procedure.

The year-by-year profile is a valuable supplement to the index rating itself because it shows the "route" traveled by Quaker (in this instance) in arriving at its 68 percentile. A similar quality profile can be drawn for, say, all food processors or any industry group. In fact, such a profile can be created for all 3000 companies in the data base. These profiles can be plotted on the same chart in order to facilitate comparisons.

TABLE 3.3   SAMPLE RANKINGS OF FIVE MIDWESTERN COMPANIES, BASED ON A WEIGHTING PROCESS

Company	Ranking	Percentile
Stewart-Warner	14444.28	73
Quaker Oats	13061.11	68
Marshall Field	11941.59	61
Sears Roebuck	11826.05	61
Jewel Companies	11770.28	60

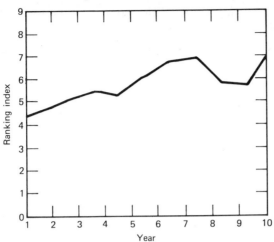

Figure 3-1. Benchmark quality profile.

Given the premise then that a universal system for measuring investment quality of common stocks is practical, what are the benefits to be derived from widespread use of such a system in the management of common stock portfolios? The most obvious benefit is the simple disclosure, to millions of stockholders, policyholders, and pension beneficiaries, of the investment quality of the financial assets being managed for them. By government decree, if not necessarily by choice, the investment industry is committed to a policy of full disclosure. If, as indicated above, investment quality measurement is both important and readily obtainable at low cost, there can be no disputing the obligation of the industry to disclose it, nor the right of beneficiaries and stockholders to receive it.

Although disclosure has a peculiarly compelling significance in the investment business, it will be recalled that the use of quality measurements in the mail-order business and in food processing is entirely voluntary. Further, the costs of measuring quality are totally absorbed by the mail-order retailer, in the one instance, and by the processors, in the other. Neither the government nor the consuming public is required to pay the cost nor demand the information. No matter how modest such costs might be, the management decision to incur them over a period of several decades must reflect a consistent conviction that there are worthwhile economic benefits. There is no reason to believe that similar benefits would not accrue in the market for common stocks.

Effective communication is the essence of the buy-sell transaction, and in the final analysis, it is the quality measurements that supply the causative data. The pictures and descriptions in the mail-order catalogue are clearly informative, but it is the quality categorization that determines the price to be paid and the buyer's willingness to pay it. People who can do so will pay a substantial premium for USDA prime beef over USDA choice if, in their minds, the price differential is matched by a quality differential. In the simplest of terms, it is the quality measurement that determines whether the price is high or low.

It naturally follows that this decision-making process is feasible only if the communication mechanism transmits information in a form that is meaningful to both buyer and seller. The term "well-marbled beef" may be meaningful to a seller but meaningless to buyers. Theoretically, a buyer could become expert in appraising beef, but it is not conceivable that he could become expert on all the products in a mail-order catalogue—or on all the common stocks available in the market. By custom and practice, the quality code "prime beef" has come to be meaningful to both buyer and seller, thus constituting a useful communication device. With effective communication of quality measurements, buyers of common stocks can be placed in a position where they too can make rational buying decisions.

Buying decisions are based on expectations that the purchase, whether by mail order, in a grocery, or from a stock broker, will satisfy what economists refer to as "a perceived need." Customers do not toss their money willy nilly into a cash register; they must be assured that the purchase will serve some purpose.

Perceived needs are created or strengthened by merchandising and promotional activities, which basically argue that the product is important to the buyer and that his perceived need will be satisfied by doing business with the seller. If the need is not satisfied, the buyer turns away—from both the product and the marketplace. Success, therefore, lies not simply in energizing the perceived need but in satisfying it as well.

It necessarily follows, then, that the seller, if he wishes to be successful, must limit the energizing of perceived needs only to those that he can satisfy. Disappointing the buyer is hazardous and not easily forgotten, particularly in the stock market, as witnessed by the four-decade separation between the 1929 and 1973 market peaks.

There is abundant evidence that buyers have become disappointed with the stock market and are withdrawing from it. According to the New York Stock Exchange, the number of investors has been dropping at the rate of 1 million per year since 1970. Mutual fund redemptions have exceeded sales for almost as long a period, since early in 1972. These trends indicate clearly that the investment industry is no longer meeting the perceived needs of many former customers.

The crux of the problem is that the merchandising efforts of the industry have for years been devoted to creating a perceived need that can be met only by accidental means. The perceived need the industry has created, and promised to deliver, is for stocks that go up in price. Yet research demonstrates that the prices of common stocks fluctuate in a random manner, making it impossible for the seller to deliver what he has promised to the buyer. In a random market, there are accidental winners as well as accidental losers so that the results are not always disastrous. Nonetheless, the recent history of withdrawals from the market necessitates a revolutionary new approach to the creation and satisfaction of perceived needs.

The key to such an approach is quality measurement. It is apparent that an industry that considers a product so bad it should be sold when it becomes available at a lower price is not allowing quality considerations to enter into the buying decision. If product quality were made known to buyers, they would become more anxious to buy stocks of a given quality when prices fell and more anxious to sell when prices rose. Only quality measurements can be effective in dividing the buying zone from the selling zone.

To the extent that there is a strategy in current investment managing and investment advising, it can be summed up as, "Dump the losers and ride with the winners." But losers and winners can be determined only after the fact, and buy-sell decisions based solely on price changes in a randomly priced market can have no rational basis. What is needed, instead, is a prudent management approach for the portfolio as a total entity, an approach that recognizes and reacts to the randomness of the market, rather than pretending to have an impossible foresight.

Such a management system can be devised by using quality measurements as other industries have done. In such a system, stocks are purchased when they are cheap, in terms of the prescribed quality standard, and sold when they become high priced. Although such a systematic management approach will not, of course, insulate a portfolio from the incidence of chance happenings, it would indeed benefit from erratic price actions.

Consistency usually involves the blending of diverse elements so that the shortage or failure of one can be compensated for by adjustments in others. Scotch whiskies, for example, are blended from a variety of grains to produce a predictably consistent drink. Blending eliminates the hope of a superior vintage, such as is possible with wines; however, while a seller can always promise delivery of satisfying Scotch whiskey, he cannot promise a vintage wine before the grapes are pressed.

The rational blending of common stocks in a portfolio can also produce consistent results—provided that the results are not measured in terms of random prices. If performance in a random market is judged by price fluctuations, there is virtually no likelihood that management in itself will produce better or worse results than random selection. It is therefore foolish to energize a perceived need on the premise that such performance can be delivered.

The rational blending of common stocks in a portfolio on the basis of quality is, by contrast, a thoroughly practical undertaking. Furthermore, when buy-sell decisions are also geared to investment yield (i.e., buy high yields, sell when they drop), it is also practical to anticipate that capital gains will be achieved with at least average success.

The perceived need that should be encouraged in such a system is an investment program that makes sense in terms of both quality and yield. Such a system is thoroughly practical, as is demonstrated in a subsequent chapter, and serves the purpose of offering a product that can be delivered as well as promised. Widespread use of such a system, whether by investors themselves or by advisers, can end the disappointments that present strategies have produced and justify the return to the marketplace of absent investors.

A shift in emphasis from illusory price increases to achievable quality/yield points as investment objectives may result from either a revision of industry attitudes or the independent recognition by investors that they must do it themselves. Because the investment industry tends to regard abandonment of the quill pen as a sufficient concession to modernization, it seems probable that the burden will have to be assumed by the investing public.

Fortunately, the operation of a quality-oriented management system is much less laborious than explaining it. This will become increasingly evident as we explore the management-by-objectives approach to administrating financial assets in the next chapter, and even more evident in the discussions of portfolio management which follow.

CHAPTER FOUR

Investment Management by Objectives

Before demonstrating the use of numerical investment quality measurements in the management of common stock portfolios, it is important to explain clearly what management-by-objectives (MBO) means and how such a system is created. Although the concept has been employed widely and successfully in the management of various work activities, its application to the management of financial assets represents a new application of these proven techniques. It is our purpose in this chapter to demonstrate that such a leap onto new ground is feasible and not frightening.

The management system described here is patterned in such a way as to make possible the application of good judgment and to measure its effects. As in most business transactions, the manager of a common stock portfolio has a bewildering array of options. The system must first lead him to focus on those areas demanding a decision, since he cannot possibly respond simultaneously to all of the options. The system must then provide a standard against which the options can be assessed and a device for measuring the results.

The key to the system is the setting of objectives, which provide the measurement tool that says a certain activity is acting badly and requires a decision and which determine that only certain alternatives are meaningful. This then clears the way for rational and deliberate decision making. It is the objectives, achieved or missed, that will ultimately demonstrate whether a decision was sound or unsound.

To illustrate the application of MBO concepts to the management of common stock portfolios, we first describe the development and workings of some other MBO systems. In doing so, we seek to identify those key elements of the system that make it successful and that can be similarly applied in portfolio management.

One of the more interesting examples of the MBO system is its use by professional football teams. All football teams have one goal—to win every game. For a considerable time, achieving that goal depended basically on hiring bigger men. Sometimes, however, the smaller teams would be faster, or try harder, or in some unpredictable manner manage a victory. Such random results made the games exciting but did little to provide job security for the coach. Accordingly, he sought to organize his available resources more effectively so as to improve the probability of winning.

Responding to this necessity, professional football teams have developed highly sophisticated MBO systems. Each player is appraised on the basis of his individual skills and assigned to a unit that can best use those skills. Each unit goes into a game knowing exactly what it is expected to achieve and how its success will be measured. The available skills are blended into a game plan that management (the coach) expects to be successful. If it is not successful, the measurement system identifies the weaknesses so that they can be corrected. The game plan is modified as needed to exploit weaknesses of opponents; hence the objectives may change from game to game.

Without necessarily being expert in the management of football teams, we can observe some of the criteria that make such a management system feasible. First, the objectives assigned to players and units must be *understandable*. Saying that the passing team must play well is of little value as an objective. Assigning a 55% pass completion rate and a 6-yard average gain states the objectives in terms that cannot be misunderstood or debated.

Second, the objectives have to be *flexible*. Each opposing team presents a new set of obstacles to success. Therefore, the blend of skills and goals has to be modified in order to improve the probability of success.

Third, the objectives must be *achievable* through the efforts of the person carrying the responsibility. Little purpose would be served by charging the safety man with responsibility for sacking the quarterback.

Fourth, the objectives must be *balanced*. Achieving a 55% completion record with a 1-yard average gain may make the quarterback look good, but isn't likely to win games.

In the final analysis, the acid test of the team's success is its ability to win games. No management system can, however, guarantee such an achievement, nor is it intended to do so. The purpose of the system is to aim at the optimum utilization of the resources available. Such resources include not only the skills of the players but also the leadership and managerial skill of the coach. If the resources are adequate, a successful result can be predicted with a high degree of probability. If the management skills are lacking, the system will make the lack clear. This may well be an unwanted benefit in the coach's eyes, but it is nonetheless one of considerable value.

The parallel between a professional football team and a business enterprise can be easily drawn. Although a business is generally made up of more numerous and larger units than is a football team, the importance of the individual units to overall success is virtually identical. The function of the management system in both instances is to blend the component units in a balanced manner so as to reach a goal.

Like a football team, a business has one basic goal. Maximizing profits is the goal of a business. We know this to be the case because the manager's bonus is conditioned on the degree of success he achieves in maximizing profits. The stockholders might wish that the goal were to maximize dividends, but such is not the case.

The business situation parallels that of the football team in that a set of intermediate objectives is required in order to improve the use of resources and to increase the probability of overall success. The objectives of an MBO system for business must meet the same criteria— understandability, flexibility, achievability, and balance.

In selecting measurements suited to an MBO system for business, painstaking study—and some trial and error—is needed to determine the measurement that best communicates the performance of the department. Some measurements that seem appropriate have to be discarded because they are not controllable by the manager. Others may not permit the flexibility needed for responding to changing circumstances. Even when the "ideal" measurement is found, the *system* is incomplete until counterbalancing objectives are also developed.

The sales activity is one instance in business where the objective can be clearly and simply stated, eliminating any possible confusion. Objectives can be set for each salesperson or store, whatever the productive unit might be, and expressed in dollar sales quotas. Assuming reasonable competence, each salesperson should be capable of achieving the objective as the result of his or her own efforts. The sales target is also flexible, since it can be modified in slow periods and revised when conditions improve.

If the production of dollar volume were the only objective for the sales activity, the sales staff's life would indeed be happy. In order to meet the enterprise's overall goal of maximizing profits, however, some balancing objectives have to be provided, even though they may tend to limit the volume of sales.

One such objective would have to deal with the credit of customers. A salesperson could undoubtedly produce a great many more sales if customers didn't have to pay their bills. Such sales don't benefit the enterprise, however; so sales have to be limited to customers with good credit histories and even then to a maximum credit balance for each account. Excessively stringent credit screening, on the other hand, would act to limit sales to an undesirable degree; accordingly, some marginal accounts have to be accepted. If there are no slow or questionable accounts, the business is probably passing up some sales. Hence, some balance must be maintained between sale targets and acceptable credit losses.

The warehousing operation provides an example of an activity where the measurement unit must be something other than dollars. The key to productivity for this department is the number of orders physically handled and shipped within a given period, usually an 8-hour shift. Accordingly, a frequently used measurement for a warehouse is one that calculates the "lines filled" during a shift, with each "line" on the order being a directive to locate, pack, and ship a certain item.

Whether in sales, collections, or warehousing, the objective must be one the manager can achieve by the way he blends the resources available to him. Varying degrees of managerial skill may be required, but that is what managers are paid to supply. Conceivably, the objective could be set so high that the manager could not achieve it, but then the objective would be valueless. Common sense dictates that the objective must be realizable if it is to perform any useful function.

As with the credit department, the sales effort and the warehouse activity must function in harmony in order to obtain overall efficiency. If monthly sales volume grows, higher output must be achieved by the warehouse or else business will be lost. Greater warehouse shipments will produce more "out-of-stock" reports unless inventories are also increased. As an object, the reduction of out-of-stock reports from 3% to 2% is specific and understandable both by the warehouse and the purchasing department.

These examples illustrate how systematic management works in directing the activities of individual departments toward an intended result and in meshing the component operations to gain the overall goal of maximizing profits. This is in keeping with the dictionary definition of a system "as a group of interacting elements forming a collective entity."

The MBO system has been extensively proven in a large variety of business situations. The question to be addressed now is how practicable is the application of such a system to the management of common stock portfolios.

The key to success in systematic business management lies in defining specific, achievable, flexible, and balanced objectives. The manager then knows what is expected of him and, sooner or later, learns to blend his own resources to achieve the desired result.

Managing a common stock portfolio also involves the blending of other resources, since it can be made up of securities drawn from thousands of possibilities. It would seem logical, therefore, that systematic management would be successful if an adequate set of numerical objectives could be developed.

It thus becomes essential that common stock portfolio be viewed as a business entity. The traditional "pick-and-pray" strategy emphasizes individual issues, hoping that one successful issue will compensate for all the deficiencies. Too often the result is a motley collection of individual issues that have been selected with little regard for the portfolio as an entity. Once the portfolio is seen as a business that can benefit from sound business management, an MBO system becomes quite practical.

One of the problems in defining investment objectives arises because the securities industry, being essentially a merchandising business, does not like to be pinned down to hard facts. Investment objectives are conventionally expressed in vague terms and are subject to widely varying interpretations. The most popular single word is "growth" because it can justify the sale of almost any kind of common stock. "Stability" is as vague as "growth" in meaning but lacks the latter's sales impact; hence, it is less popular. "Income stock" is one of the more informative, and least used, phrases, but it is not defined numerically.

Although little use is made of "income stock," it can readily be expressed numerically. The appropriate calculation is the relationship between the cost of the investment and the dividend received during the year, which is known as the *yield*. A stock costing $10.00 and paying a $.50 dividend has a yield of 5%. If the dividend goes up to $.60, the yield becomes 6%. On the other hand, a stock costing $12.00 and paying a $.60 dividend, also has a yield of 5%. Thus yield can well serve as an understandable and flexible objective, if it is simply stated in numerical terms, for example, 5%.

The level at which a yield objective should be set depends largely on the goal of the investment program. An insurance company contracts with its policyholders to provide a guaranteed return; its investment portfolio then must be managed to produce at least such a yield. Maximum effort is put into maintaining the reliability of the yield. Little benefit would be derived from the extra income of a higher yield because the risk must also be higher. The investment manager produces the required result by blending the yields from all the resources available to him, including bonds and common stocks.

In order to be managed, a common stock portfolio (or any portfolio) must have a purpose. The purpose of an insurance company portfolio is quite likely different from that of a pension trust or a mutual fund. Among individual investors, there may well be a number of different purposes.

If yield is to be used effectively as an objective in a portfolio management system, the yield objective must be clearly stated and consistent with the overall purpose. The popular phrase "maximum yield consistent with maximum safety" is totally without meaning—no one can intelligently define either maximum yield or maximum safety.

The businesslike approach to setting a yield objective is to correlate it with the portfolio purpose. If an insurance company guarantees a 5% return, it would seem to make sense that the yield objective should approximate 5%, not "whatever we can get." A pension fund should be able to forecast its future cash needs with some degree of reliability and work this backward into an objective. A mutual fund is obliged to express its investment objectives as clearly as possible, and the managers are paid to achieve them.

Individual investors may have to devote considerable thought to selecting a yield objective. They must review the returns they are currently obtaining through insurance and retirement benefits. They must also weigh the alternative yields available to them, from savings accounts, for example. If their circumstances change, they may choose to modify their yield objectives.

Once the yield objective has been set, developing the management system requires that a second objective be set up as a balancing force. As pointed out earlier, all systems involve at least two objectives which tend to be counterbalancing; it is the balancing of the objectives which produces desired results.

Business management of a portfolio is no exception. Even if a relatively modest yield is specified, the human tendency is to seek maximization of the yield without regard to other concerns. This is particularly true if the manager expects his own performance to be judged on the yield alone. Since yields tend to reach a maximum just before disappearing (caused by omitting dividend payments), it is clear that some balancing objective must be brought into play.

As pointed out in the preceding chapters, it is the thesis here that investment quality can serve as the essential second objective for a management system. Like yield, investment quality is a mathematical statement about a common stock portfolio which specifies a measurable "property" of the portfolio and of the issues in it.

This is not to say that other objectives might not also meet the essential criteria. A similar numerical approach is feasible, for example, with the price-earning ratio. For the present purpose, however, the system objectives used in this discussion will be limited to yield and investment quality.

In order to illustrate the use of yield and quality measurements in a portfolio management system, we will assume that objectives have been assigned or selected to maintain quality at 6500 (on a scale of 100 to 9900) and yield at 4%. In order to achieve these objectives, we have constructed the portfolio listed below. Note that quality is expressed by the Benchmark® Index Number, which is expressed in two digits for individual companies but four digits for the portfolio.

Co.	Investment	Quality	Dividend	Yield
A	$10,000	75	$ 300	3.0%
B	10,000	70	350	3.5
C	10,000	65	400	4.0
D	10,000	60	450	4.5
E	10,000	55	500	5.0
Total	$50,000	6500	$2,000	4.0%

It should be noted that the quality and yield totals for the portfolio represent weighted averages. Simplified methods for making these calculations are set forth in the Appendix.

For clarity, the quality/yield coordinate for each stock and for the portfolio can be plotted on a chart. The portfolio objective thus becomes the "Benchmark" by which the suitability of each issue is measured.

The portfolio shown above clearly meets the assigned objectives of quality and yield, 6500 and 4% respectively, by blending stocks with a range of both quality and yield. The need for management arises when fluctuations in stock prices change the symmetry which is shown above. Not a great deal is known about the movement of common stock prices but one can always expect that they will fluctuate. The task of the manager is to respond to such fluctuations; the function of the management system is to improve his ability to so respond.

It is probable that prices of all five of the stocks will change some-

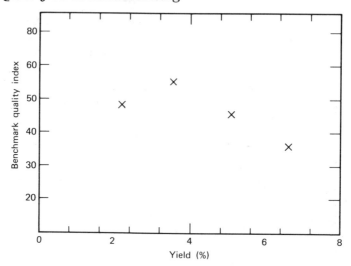

Figure 4A-10. Quality/yield chart.

what in any given period of time but, in order to illustrate the function-ing of the system, we will consider only one change at a time.

As an initial example, let us assume that the market price of stock A has gone up 20% in price. We say that the investment then is $12,000 since we have not converted the apparent realizable value into cash and are foregoing the alternate use of it. Because of the higher invest-ment, the yield on this particular issue drops to 2.5% since the divi-dend itself hasn't changed.

The effect on the *portfolio* objective of this price change is to re-duce the yield to 3.8% and to increase the quality index to 6538. Hence, the change in market price for this stock has brought about a situation where the portfolio is no longer meeting its objective.

The system thus is notifying the manager that a decision is called for in order to bring the portfolio back into conformity with its objec-tives. The problem area is clearly defined since it is stock A which is pulling the portfolio away from its benchmark. Presumably, a 3.0% yield was tolerable for stock A when the overall blend produced a yield of 4.0%; the manager must now decide what to do about stock A to restore the balance.

One logical option would be to liquidate the $2,000 of apparent gain and transfer the proceeds to stock E, where it would purchase $100 of additional dividends. Such an action would also shift the quality index downward, toward the benchmark. The actual result would be a quality index of 6462 and a portfolio yield of 3.94%, just slightly below target.

The manager might choose instead to transfer funds from stock A to stock C, or to some other stock with the same quality/yield coordinate. This would maintain quality at the 6500 level but would rebuild the yield only to 3.90%.

It is clear that the system is advising the manager that some action should be taken if the objectives are to be met, and that the action must be centered on stock A. He is free to evaluate the options and to select the one which he finds preferable. The system also enables him to measure the impact of his decision on the overall objectives. A series of "what-if" calculations can guide his decision, or he can calculate mathematically how much to invest in, say, stock E in order to meet the objective.

Without going through all of the arithmetic, it can be seen that an increase in the price of stock E would pull the quality index *down* and also reduce the yield, again pulling the portfolio away from its benchmark. Thus, the manager would have a different set of circumstances to which he must respond but, again, the focus and impact of his judgment are clearly defined.

Not all changes in stock prices are upward, as many investors have learned; hence, the system must also be able to react to price declines. Thus, if the price of stock A dropped significantly, the quality index would fall but the yield would improve. The manager would then have still another set of circumstances to which he had to respond and his decisions would necessarily be different. The system itself, however, would again signal the need for a decision, would focus clearly on the stock (or stocks) for which a decision was required, and would similarly measure the impact of the decision.

This illustration is highly simplified but does serve to illustrate the functioning of the management system. Briefly stated, any significant change in market prices distorts the desired interrelationship between quality and yield. The system signals the occurrence of the distortion, identifies the cause and encourages the manager to take specific corrective action.

The foregoing example is intended merely to illustrate the options which become available to a manager when stock prices change. A more complex management exercise can be studied by using a portfolio made up of the 30 stocks which comprise the Dow Jones Industrial Average, assuming ownership of 100 shares in each issue. Such a portfolio might look like this:

Company	Investment	Quality	Div.	Yield
Allied Chemical	$ 3,950	72	$180	4.6%
Alcoa	5,800	39	140	2.4
Am. Brands	4,100	88	280	6.8
Am. Can	3,525	67	220	6.2
A T T	5,975	73	380	6.4
Beth. Steel	3,950	46	200	5.1
Chrysler	2,100	62	60	2.9
Du Pont	13,625	88	425	3.1
Eastman	9,650	87	156	1.8
Esmark	3,200	35	152	4.7
Exxon	5,300	86	280	5.3
G E	5,575	87	160	2.9
G M	6,700	94	315	4.7
Gen. Foods	3,250	71	150	4.6
Goodyear	2,300	46	110	4.8
Int. Harvester	3,075	63	170	5.5
Int. Paper	6,550	73	200	3.0
Inco	3,400	90	160	4.7
Johns-Manville	2,950	58	140	4.7
M M M	6,250	83	145	2.3
Owens-Illinois	5,800	41	188	3.2
P & G	9,300	82	220	2.4
Sears	6,500	68	160	2.5
Std. Calif.	3,800	76	220	5.8
Texaco	2,725	84	200	7.3
Un. Carbide	6,400	77	250	3.9
United Techs.	3,500	58	120	3.4
U. S. Steel	5,025	50	220	4.4
Westinghouse	1,700	59	97	5.7
Woolworth	2,250	50	120	5.3

For purposes of this exercise, we will again assume that the designated benchmark is 6500/4, an index of quality set at 6500 and the yield at 4%.

Based upon the market prices reflected in the "Investment" column, the index of quality for this portfolio works out to 7219 and the yield at 3.92%. Thus, the portfolio is on target in terms of yield but is too high on the quality scale.

It should be clearly understood that use of a 4% yield objective in this illustration is not to be interpreted as an endorsement of such a yield level as an objective. Suitability of such an objective is a decision to be made by each portfolio beneficiary.

Proceeding on the assumption that the 4% yield is satisfactory, however, the quality/yield test can be used to categorize the issues in this portfolio in terms of the stated objective as follows:

Satisfactory yield

Good quality (A):

Allied Chemical	72	4.6%
Am. Brands	88	6.8
Am. Can	67	6.2
A T T	73	6.4
Exxon	86	5.3
G M	94	4.7
Gen. Foods	71	4.6
Inco	90	4.7
Std. Calif.	76	5.8
Texaco	84	7.3

Medium quality (B):

Beth. Steel	46	5.1
Esmark	35	4.7
Goodyear	46	4.8
U. S. Steel	50	4.4
Woolworth	50	5.3

Borderline situations (C):

Int. Harvester	63	5.5
Johns Manville	58	4.7
Union Carbide	77	3.9
Westinghouse	59	5.7

Below-target yield

High quality (D):

DuPont	88	3.1
Eastman	87	1.8
G E	87	2.9
Int. Paper	73	3.0
M M M	83	2.3
P & G	82	2.4
Sears	68	2.5

Medium quality (E):

Alcoa	58	2.4
Chrysler	62	2.9
Owens-Illinois	41	3.2
United Techs.	58	3.4

The issues fall into five categories, each demanding a different kind of attention (or inattention) from the manager. Rather than being faced with 30 separate decisions, the manager is in a position to focus his judgment on only those issues demanding an investment decision.

For example, it can be seen that the stocks in categories A, B, and C do not demand immediate attention. Thus the manager's area of concern has been focused by the system on the seven issues in category D and the four in category E. Since the category E stocks fail to meet portfolio standards of either quality or yield, they can quickly be classified as "sales" so as to make funds available for investments which do meet the objectives.

The system has, in essence then, reduced the manager's concern from potentially 30 buy-sell decisions to the seven issues in category D. His ultimate actions about these securities are not critical to the functioning of the system, which has done its primary job in bringing these few issues to his attention as demanding a decision. The same measurement system that permitted this result will also measure the impact of his decisions, before he makes them if he chooses to calculate the "what if" impacts on the portfolio, and certainly after he has done so.

The foregoing exercises clearly demonstrate that an MBO system based on quality/yield relationships is feasible for portfolio management. What every one wants to know, however, is not just whether the system can function but what benefit will result if it is effectively employed. Since "benefit" is almost always described as the production of paper profits, that is the issue to be considered.

The research literature consistently emphasizes the random nature of changes in stock prices. If the market pricing of common stocks is truly and inevitably a random process, it necessarily follows that no management system will do better or worse than any other system. There can be short-term exceptions due to accidental events, but that conclusion cannot be disputed if the stock market is truly random.

The function of the quality/yield system is to direct management toward the *purchase* of a stream of income having a known quality when the market price is low, and toward the *sale* of that income stream when the market price is high. The uninterrupted functioning of such a system, assuming it is intelligently operated, cannot fail to produce both a specified income level and some capital gains. What cannot be predicted is the time span for the realization of gains; the inevitable result of buying low and selling high, however, is obvious.

The central fact here, however, is that the production of paper profits is not relevant to prudent investing. The investment industry emphasizes paper profits because it receives real money from them; the owners do not. What needs to be understood is that the investment industry stands virtually alone among business enterprises in its total and unremitting disdain for quality control, an essential element in any management system.

As is shown in the pages that follow, quality-oriented portfolio management is a practical means whereby even part-time investors can order their own priorities, whether they are quality, income, or capital gains. Further, they can do so with the peace of mind that comes from knowing what they are doing.

CHAPTER FIVE

Working Up to Portfolio Management

Investing in common stocks, when compared with investing in a savings account or in government bonds, is a high-risk undertaking. It is important to add that it is less of a high-risk undertaking than playing a slot machine or gambling in Las Vegas or, indeed, in contrast with many other forms of speculation. Nonetheless, the purchase of common stocks puts at risk whatever amount of money is involved, and rational investors should approach such an enterprise with a reasonable degree of caution.

This is not, of course, to suggest that common stock investing should be avoided simply because it is a relatively high-risk undertaking. Quite clearly, we all normally engage in high-risk activities which endanger not simply our money but our lives. During the course of a Sunday afternoon drive, we put our lives on the line dozens of times as oncoming cars pass within inches of us. The simple rule that neither crosses the yellow line encourages us to risk our lives in this fashion and, so long as the rules are observed, nobody suffers.

Not everyone is contented with Sunday driving, which is admittedly a fairly tame occupation, as indicated by the interest in the Indianapolis 500 and similar activities. However, it should be pointed out that only 33 people drive in the 500 and that they do not carry passengers. Furthermore, they, too, are subjected to very stringent rules, in many ways more stringent than those that concern the Sunday driver.

Rational investing, therefore, tends to be identified more correctly with Sunday driving than with the Indianapolis 500 and is basically not intended to provide excitement. What is needed is a business-like use of those financial assets that are available for common stock investing, employing them in such a manner as to produce a realistic probability of future profits. Such a course of action can produce both peace of mind and a reasonable return on the capital employed. There is no suggestion that this is the only way to make money through investing, and those who feel confident of their ability to speculate aggressively and successfully are certainly encouraged to do so.

In this chapter we are concentrating on methods of developing both a reasonable pool of capital with which to work and the investment skills needed to manage such capital effectively. Our beginning assumption is that the investor has a small amount of capital and few investment skills; hence, we outline a program to help him develop these assets before he assumes management responsibility for a common stock portfolio.

The first rule that we should like to propose is that funds set aside for common stock investing should be, to the maximum extent practical, set aside solely for this purpose. Admittedly, it is difficult to presume that any portion of a person's financial assets is untouchable in times of emergency. Nonetheless, it is equally difficult to set about the management of a pool of assets unless there is a reasonable assurance that all the assets will continue to be available to the manager.

The basic purpose of systematized management is to focus decision making and to measure the results of it. If decisions have to be undertaken on the basis of needs other than those encompassed in the management problem (such a need as emergency cash withdrawals for example), it is unrealistic to expect good results. For example, buying a stock with the expectation that it will mature in 3 or 4 years is a reasonable decision, but if the manager is forced to liquidate the investment in 12 months, the decision becomes meaningless.

In the discussion that follows, it has accordingly been assumed that the amount of money available for the investing project has been totally isolated. Accordingly, no amounts of money are set aside for emergency purposes, and the premise is that all of the funds referred to are available specifically and entirely for common stock investing. It is also assumed that these funds represent debt-free assets and that they will not be withdrawn from the common stock fund in order to meet debt payments. The rationale here is virtually the same; investment decisions have little meaning if they are overturned by the need to pay back debt. Borrowing money in order to buy stocks passes control over the assets to the lender and makes it impossible to carry through a managed investment program. At the same time, borrowing money for common stock investment makes it easily possible to lose the entire amount of money invested—an eventuality that is virtually impossible except when borrowed money is used.

We also strongly recommend that a common stock investment program not be initiated until there are funds available to achieve a reasonable degree of diversification. Investing in common stocks involves probabilities, not certainties, and undue risk is assumed if all the assets are invested in a single issue. The exception, which is discussed shortly, is investing in the common stock of a diversified investment company which provides diversification in itself. In terms of direct investing, however, the risk can be brought down to tolerable proportions if the investing program is not initiated until it is possible to acquire four or five stocks. By the same token, a combination of investment company shares and direct investing can provide reasonable diversification.

The folklore of the securities business can be counted on to generate stories of investors who bought a single stock and skyrocketed to wealth on that single issue. These legends are often condensed in the axiom to "Put all your eggs in one basket and then watch the basket carefully." The author of that axiom, however, didn't simply watch the basket; he controlled every activity involved with it. The holder of 100 shares of common stocks, however, is not in any position to control the activities surrounding his basket. The diversification principle, therefore, says that one should not put all of his eggs in one basket.

Accepting the premise that a planned investment program should not be initiated until funds are available for a diversified portfolio, the natural question is, what to do in the interim? Not everyone starts out with the $25,000 or $30,000 required to acquire a diversified portfolio, but people with fewer funds are certainly entitled to invest in common stocks. The suggested interim device is to invest in investment companies, of which there are many, in order to obtain both a diversification of risk and to develop some skills by observing the management of these funds.

Investment companies are basically of two types. One is the so-called mutual fund, which is technically described as an open-end company. This means that the investment company itself is the sole market for its shares, selling them either directly or through a distributor network, and repurchasing the shares whenever the owners decide they no longer want to be a part of the business. The other type is the closed-end investment company, which sells shares from time to time (as does any corporation) in order to raise capital. The shares are then traded on the stock exchanges or in the over-the-counter market in a usual fashion. Mutual funds are by far the more popular of the two forms of investment companies, with assets probably 10 times as great as those managed by the closed-end companies.

The major reason for the difference in popularity is that 8–9% of the money supplied to the open-end companies by their owners is dedicated to marketing the shares. By contrast, the closed-end companies, after the initial offering, provide marketing compensation to the sales staff in the area of 1%. It isn't difficult to imagine which of these shares will be more popular with the sales staff.

There is a third type of marketing which should also be noted, the so-called no-load mutual fund. This is an open-end investment company that buys and sells its own shares; however, it pays no sales commission to the brokers or sales staff who promote sales. Rather, the no-load funds try to develop their business through conventional advertising and sales promotion techniques, rather than personal selling.

Despite the greater popularity of the mutual funds, it is recommended here that the beginning investor make his initial investments in closed-end companies. Most such companies are listed on the New York Stock Exchange and other major exchanges; hence, they are freely available for purchase and can be sold just as easily. If the ultimate goal is active management of a common stock portfolio, the initiative to buy investment company shares, or any other shares, should rest with the manager and not the sales staff. Thus, we see the purchase of closed-end company stocks as a means of developing additional capital and the decision to purchase as initiating a learning process, which will ultimately lead to direct management of the common stock portfolio.

There is one other consideration of major importance which distinguishes the closed-end companies from the mutual funds: mutual funds, by and large, are managed by investment advisors who also are managing many other funds of various kinds. Some closed-end companies are also managed on a fee basis by similar concerns, but a number of closed-end companies are directly managed by the officers of the issuing corporation.

The management of a large number of accounts by a single agency presents an irreconcilable conflict of interest. Whenever a decision is reached that some action should be taken with regard to a specific issue of securities, whether to sell or to buy, the manager of 100 or 1000 accounts must immediately set up a priority list of customers who will get preferential treatment. Only in the case of very small accounts is it even conceivable that all the investment actions flowing from the decision can be executed simultaneously. Thus the manager is unable to treat all of his customers equally.

Because an investment company operates on a closed-end basis does not in itself guarantee that management is internal, to use the technical phrase. Several of the closed-end companies also operate with advisors running the business on a fee basis. The simplest way to distinguish between these two types of management arrangements is to look at the income and expense statement, which will show an item of "salaries" if the management is internal or "management fees" if an advisor is used.

Perhaps the basic decision to be faced is whether the investor wants 100% of the management's attention concentrated on the use of his money or whether he can be satisfied with some unknown percentage of the management's efforts and interest.

For purposes of illustration in this discussion, we have selected four closed-end companies—Adams Express Co., Madison Funds, Inc., Niagara Share Corporation, and United States and Foreign Securities Corp. (see Table 5.1)—all of which are internally managed. All four of the companies are listed on the New York Stock Exchange as well as other exchanges. Because the Benchmark management system defines its objectives in terms of investment quality and yield, we have accordingly calculated the Benchmark Index of investment quality for each of the companies. The yield, based on market prices as of December 31, 1975, and the dividend for the year ended, is shown in Table 5.2. It will be seen from the table that even this small sampling provides a considerable degree of diversity in terms of both the Benchmark Index and the yield. The index ranges from a low of 4512 to 6159, while the yield ranges from 2.4% to 6.4%. When plotted on a quality/yield chart, the four issues appear as shown in Figure 5.1.

TABLE 5.1   FOUR CLOSED-END INVESTMENT COMPANIES

Company	Number of Stockholders
Adams Express Company	30,495
Madison Fund, Inc.	81,190
Niagara Share Corporation	9,354
United States and Foreign Securities Corp.	8,700

TABLE 5.2   YIELD OF FOUR OPEN-END INVESTMENT COMPANIES, BASED ON DIVIDEND FOR YEAR ENDED DECEMBER 31, 1975

Company	Benchmark Index	Price (December 31, 1975)	Yield (%)
Adams Express	5512	10⅛	4.8
Madison Fund, Inc.	4512	9⅜	6.4
Niagara Share Corporation	5940	12⅜	2.4
United States and Foreign Securities Corp.	6159	14⅞	3.8

In discussing these four companies as prospective investment vehicles, we are not necessarily recommending these securities as investments. Any such recommendation would have to be based on the price at the time of the investment and the individual needs of the investor. Our primary purpose here is to illustrate a plan for developing an understanding of these businesses preparatory to reaching an investment decision about them.

The most effective way to begin developing an understanding of a business is to write to the corporate office and request a recent annual report and prospectus. Since the investor is probably not going to make a decision immediately, it is advisable to ask that his name be put on the mailing list for materials that are ordinarily sent to stockholders. This is a courtesy that is commonly extended for a limited period of time to prospective purchasers of shares. Although a fair amount of information may be forthcoming as the result of such a request, we concentrate this discussion on the annual report to the stockholders and suggest some methods for analyzing such a report.

The first thing to do in analyzing an annual report is to study the certificate prepared by independent certified public accountants. This is usually toward the back of the report and may take some searching to locate. There is little purpose, however, in reading the rest of the report until the certificate has been examined. It is based on an audit of the corporation's financial position and prepared by an independent auditing firm selected by the board of directors to act on behalf of the owners of the corporation. After such an audit, the independent auditors can usually state something like the following:

In our opinion, the financial statements present fairly the financial position of [the company] at December 31, 19–, and the results of its operations and changes in assets for the year then ended, in conformity with generally accepted accounting principles applied on a consistent basis.

This certificate is the auditor's way of saying that the records of the company are in good order and that the financial statements are not misleading or inaccurate. If such a certificate is not in the annual report, or if the certificate has qualifying sentences that explain why the auditors cannot prepare a similar certificate, the investor must decide whether he wants to spend any further time studying the company. In most instances, the answer to that proposition would be negative. The four investment companies we are concerned with had valid certificates in their 1975 reports so the question does not arise here.

The second thing to do in analyzing an annual report is to study the notes to the financial statements. These again are prepared by the independent auditing firm. In general, these notes cover such areas of information as the basis for valuing the assets of the business, the tax status of the corporation, compensation paid to related officers and directors, and any special items that, in the auditor's view, need clarification.

With a single exception, the notes in the annual reports of the four investment companies are common and require no special comment. The exception is the United States and Foreign Securities Corp., which has some minor investments in so-called restricted securities (stocks not registered under Securities and Exchange Commission regulations). This means that those investments cannot be readily sold, which could be a significant problem if the amounts were large.

In all four annual reports the notes state that the corporations are registered investment companies. This means, among other things, that they do not pay corporate tax so long as they distribute 90% of their earnings to the owners. Further, they must meet certain diversification standards.

Having established through the foregoing process that the financial statements are worth study, the next logical step is to look at the balance sheet. The purpose of the balance sheet is to inform the reader, first, of how much money the management was provided to manage and, second, how those funds were put to work. The key to success in any business is how effectively the management uses the assets made available to it. Thus, the first step in comparing similar businesses is to learn how the capital was obtained and how the money was used.

The amount and source of the assets which the managers of the

TABLE 5.3   AMOUNT AND SOURCE OF ASSETS

(*in millions*)

Company	Sale of Shares	Retained Surplus	Total
Adams Express	$146,966	$ 8,243	$155,209
Madison Fund	367,902	(1,434)	366,468
Niagara Share	30,607	34,069	64,676
United States and Foreign Securities Corp.	73,026	9,594	82,620

four companies had available for use at December 31, 1975, are shown in Table 5.3. The information is taken from Statement of Capital Shares and Surplus in the annual report. The first column in Table 5.3 shows the amount of money brought into the business through the sale of stock to the original owners; this clearly is the major source of capital for each of the businesses. The second column, Retained Surplus, is modest because, as noted previously, registered investment companies are called on to distribute virtually all of their earnings to the owners. The surplus figures include both regular earned and retained income and capital gains or losses. Thus it is feasible for Madison Fund to show a negative surplus figure by taking capital losses, even though it is generating current income.

Included in the Statement of Capital Shares and Surplus is the item Unrealized Appreciation or Depreciation on Investments. This represents the difference between the cost of the investments and the apparent market value as of the balance sheet date. Since these are not useable assets until they are converted into cash and since our concern is with management's use of assets, they have been excluded from Table 5.3.

The reason for existence of these businesses, as with any other business, is the expectation that the management will use the assets in such a way as to produce something beneficial for the owners. In the case of an investment company, there are two basic benefits:

1. A current investment income paid out as dividends.
2. Realized capital gains that are distributed to the owners.

TABLE 5.4   RELATIONSHIP OF INVESTMENT INCOME TO INVESTED CAPITAL, 1975

(*in millions*)

Company	Investment Income	Invested Capital	% Return
Adams Express	$7,141	$155,209	4.6
Madison Fund	8,782	366,468	2.4
Niagara Share	1,742	64,676	2.7
United States and Foreign Securities Corp.	2,774	82,620	3.4

In comparing these four companies, therefore, it is important to see how well the managers have succeeded in producing one or both of the benefits.

Looking initially to the development of investment income, Table 5.4 shows the relationship of the 1975 investment income to the invested capital for each of the four companies. As can be seen from the table, there is a considerable disparity in the ratio of available assets to the income generated by the various managements. In order to gain insight into these differences, it is appropriate to start with the beginning point and compare the gross return on investments to the invested capital, as shown in Table 5.5. Again, there is considerable disparity in these gross yields, although the managements have all been dealing in the same marketplace and have had identical investment opportunities available to them.

Naturally, the difference between the gross income and the net

TABLE 5.5   GROSS RETURN ON INVESTMENT

Adams Express	5.3%
Madison Fund	3.0
Niagara Share	4.0
United States and Foreign Securities Corp.	4.9

investment income represents the expenses disbursed in managing the business. Thus the next analytical step is to calculate the expense ratio for the four companies, as shown in Table 5.6. It should be noted that commissions on buying and selling stocks are recorded only as part of the purchase (or sale) transaction; hence, it is never possible to determine how much these disbursements total.

It is apparent from Table 5.6 that there is some economy in size in this type of business, inasmuch as the two smaller funds have significantly higher expense ratios than the larger funds. Nonetheless, the difference in the expense ratios does not fully explain the difference in the net investment return; hence, it can be concluded that Madison Fund and Niagara Share have deliberately chosen to accept a lower investment return objective. The alternative conclusion would be that their managers are incapable of achieving a return comparable to that of Adams Express and United States and Foreign Securities Corp.

In order to provide some perspective for these percentage return figures, it should be noted that the average return earned by major noninvestment corporations in 1975 was 11.2%. And the returns themselves range as high as 18.9% for the drug industry and 21.8% for companies in the oil service and supply business. These industries produce a high rate of return on invested capital as a normal process and the rates are substantially higher when compared with the investment companies. Therefore, the use of investment company shares for personal investment should, in most instances, be an interim step toward the direct management of a portfolio made up of shares in operating companies.

TABLE 5.6 EXPENSE RATIOS, 1975

(*in millions*)

Company	Gross Income	Expenses	Expense Ratio (%)
Adams Express	$ 8,277	$1,136	13.7
Madison Fund	10,852	2,070	19.1
Niagara Share	2,604	862	33.1
United States and Foreign Securities Corp.	4,021	1,248	31.0

The second benefit that the owners can derive from an investment company is the distribution of capital gains. Such a benefit is rarely practical for the owners of an industrial corporation because the assets of such a business lack the liquidity available to an investment company.

As a general rule, the investment companies take capital gains during the year, at times which seem appropriate to the managers, and pay out a supplementary capital gains distribution once a year. The relationship of such distributions during 1975 to the invested capital for the four companies is shown in Table 5.7. It can be seen that Madison Fund took some capital losses during this period, which is an option available to the managers if their judgment indicates that such losses should be taken.

Using the combined total of investment income and capital gains distributions, a more respectable return is—in most instances—recorded by the four investment companies, as shown in Table 5.8. An important contributing factor to the profitability of the investment company is the extent to which it has its funds invested in working assets. At any given point in time, the management may feel that it is appropriate to withdraw from the stock market and hold cash reserves instead. For this reason, it is generally sound practice to calculate the extent to which each investment company has its funds invested in common stocks and investment securities, as opposed to cash and other assets, as shown in Table 5.9. In the case of these four companies, there is no great differential between them in terms of their asset usage. However, if one such fund should, for example, have only 60%

TABLE 5.7   RELATIONSHIP OF GAINS DISTRIBUTION TO INVESTED CAPITAL, 1975

(*in millions*)

Company	Realized Gains	Invested Capital	% Return
Adams Express	$5,690	$155,209	3.7
Madison Fund	(3,028)	366,468	(0.8)
Niagara Share	4,828	64,676	7.5
United States and Foreign Securities Corp.	2,777	82,620	3.4

TABLE 5.8   COMBINED TOTAL OF INVESTMENT INCOME AND CAPITAL
GAINS DISTRIBUTIONS

Company	Investment Income (%)	Capital Gains Distribution (%)	Total (%)
Adams Express	4.6	3.7	8.3
Madison Fund	2.4	(0.8)	1.6
Niagara Share	2.7	7.5	10.2
United States and Foreign Securities Corp.	3.4	3.4	6.8

of its assets invested in securities, clearly the rate of return on capital
would have to be scrutinized in a different light.

Because the closed-end investment company has no obligation
to buy back its own shares of stock, as do mutual funds, it is not necessary for closed-end companies to maintain cash reserves for this purpose. Although the mutual funds may also choose to maintain cash
reserves as a result of investment decisions, they must keep cash available as well to meet redemption requests. This has been particularly
true in recent years, since redemptions of mutual fund shares have
generally exceeded their sales. Some representative mutual fund per-

TABLE 5.9   PERCENT OF FUNDS INVESTED

(*in millions*)

Company	Total Assets	Other Assets	% Invested
Adams Express	$158,727	$22,282	86
Madison Fund	369,126	9,241	97
Niagara Share	65,142	6,735	90
United States and Foreign Securities Corp.	85,402	8,889	90

centages of investment securities held to total assets are shown in Table 5.10.

The need for extra liquidity that the mutual fund managers must face may also inhibit their investment in businesses requiring time to mature. As noted earlier, the possible necessity for withdrawing cash from the common stock portfolio makes it unreasonable to invest in situations that may take 3 or 4 years to mature.

One of the principal objectives in acquiring shares of an investment company is diversification. For example, the purchaser of 100 shares of each of the four investment companies at December 31, 1975, would have had to invest roughly $4700. That sum of money could scarcely be diversified into even two or three issues without paying heavy commission costs for odd-lot transactions, those involving less than 100 shares. If invested in the four investment companies, however, that same $4700 would have purchased a proportionate interest in a large number of issues, as shown in Table 5.11. The diversification index is a simple calculation made to relate the number of issues to the total size of the fund. As can be seen in Table 5.11, all four companies represent a considerable diversification, although Madison Fund is at the lower end of the scale. For comparison purposes, similar diversification index numbers for some major mutual funds are shown in Table 5.12.

It will be recalled that we suggested the acquisition of investment shares as a means of building capital during an interim period. These companies offer a convenient way of adding to this investment through an automatic dividend reinvestment plan and a voluntary cash purchase plan. In effect, this program enables the owner to acquire addi-

TABLE 5.10 SAMPLE MUTUAL FUND PERCENT OF INVESTMENT SECURITIES HELD TO TOTAL ASSETS

Mutual Fund	%
Axe Houghton Stock Fund	73
Comstock Fund	81
I D S Progressive Fund	59
Keystone Growth Fund	75
Putnam Growth Fund	75

TABLE 5.11   NUMBER OF ISSUES PURCHASED BY INVEST-
ING $4700 IN THE FOUR INVESTMENT COMPANIES

Company	Issues	Diversification Index
Adams Express	98	60
Madison Fund	105	36
Niagara Share	50	95
United States and Foreign Securities Corp.	73	78

tional shares without paying a commission. There is ordinarily a small service charge, which seems to run about $.60 per transaction.

It is conventional for investment companies to show the effectiveness of an automatic reinvestment program by tracing the growth of an initial investment of an assumed amount of money. One point that is not shown in these tables, but which should be clearly understood, is that the owner must pay the tax on the distributions when they are recorded, even though he doesn't receive the funds. The effect, of course, is that his total investment consists both of the monies left with the investment company and the taxes paid.

In purchasing closed-end investment company shares, the investor takes the same market risks that go with direct investing. The shares of

TABLE 5.12   DIVERSIFICATION INDEX NUMBERS FOR
SEVERAL MAJOR MUTUAL FUNDS

Mutual Fund	Diversification Index
Chemical Fund	14
Fidelity Fund	18
Investment Company of America	14
Massachusetts Investors Trust	7
Technology Fund	20

the four investment companies are listed on the New York Stock Exchange, and the price will vary from time to time. Such variations reflect the ebb and flow of popularity for this type of investment and for the presumed competence of the individual managements.

While we recommend investing in these types of investment companies primarily in order to build capital for a direct investment program, this interim period can also be used for developing individual investment skill. As will be seen in the following discussion, techniques similar to those used in studying the four investment companies are also useful in preparing for a direct investment program.

An important theme running through this discussion of the Benchmark management system is the requirement that the investor maintain full control over decision making. This was noted in explaining the benefit of segregating funds for common stock investing and of avoiding debt for investment purposes. The emphasis on closed-end investment companies is similar in concept; typically, these shares are "purchased" while mutual fund shares are actively "sold" by aggressive salespeople. The impetus toward the purchase is provided by the buyer rather than the salesperson.

It may appear that we are placing undue emphasis on the origin of investment decisions, whether it be buyer or salesperson. The hard fact, however, is that one must choose between being the "victim" of someone else's decision making or being the instigator of one's own decisions. This choice is usually obscured by the assertion that recommendations by salespeople are not decisive and that the ultimate decision is left to the investor. In point of fact, investment recommendations are usually made to persons without an ability to evaluate them. Under such circumstances, the recommendation is the decision; only the formality of signing a check separates them. It is within this frame of reference that we recommend strongly the development of an independent decision-making capability.

Unplanned investing more often than not results from an impetus provided by a salesperson. This is particularly true of investors who cannot spend their full time on their investing business. In a typical transaction, the broker calls with an idea or a new offering of stock. Common stock purchases are largely handled by telephone; the investor hasn't even the time needed to write a check in order to think through his commitment. There is almost always some pressure to act quickly, either because the price is "certain" to rise or because there won't be enough stock to go around for everyone. Such pressure tends to lessen the investor's control over the decision making.

One method of relieving such pressures is to develop an "approved" list of stocks and limit purchases to securities on the list. This technique is employed by most major investing institutions and can be just as useful for an individual investor. Within the context of the present discussion, developing an approved list can also be looked on as a valuable learning experience that doesn't cost money. Learning to invest while using real money can be very expensive. Developing an approved list provides an opportunity to study a number of companies without risking capital.

Keeping in mind that a fair amount of time may be needed to develop a pool of capital, a lengthy period can be allocated to establishing an approved list. During this time, the investor can learn his own strengths and weaknesses—again, without risking capital. Individual aptitudes are inherent in the investing process, as well as in other activities, and it is preferable to learn these before putting real money at risk.

The one aptitude all investors would like to have is an unerring ability to identify stocks that immediately double or triple in price. If there are people with such a skill, they don't waste time reading books such as this one. In a practical sense, other aptitudes are of real importance. Some individuals may find themselves skilled in identifying young companies at an early growth stage. Others may be strong in evaluating technology, while still another group may be best at evaluating financially oriented businesses in banking or insurance.

It is certainly as important to identify weaknesses as strengths, and to acknowledge them. If an investor finds himself consistently making errors with regard to a certain type of company, he is better off to forget that category. Since there are literally thousands of stocks to select from, it should not be a problem to tailor a list that emphasizes the investor's strengths, not his weaknesses.

Candidates for consideration can be picked from numerous sources. Appendix B to this book lists several hundred companies, showing a Benchmark Index Number for each. Although it is not possible for this list of index numbers to be current while the book is in print, they do provide a general order of quality ranking from which portfolio candidates can be drawn.

Another source of potential candidates will be the investment company portfolios. Assuming the investor has purchased shares in one or more of the companies discussed previously, he will have a list of perhaps 100 names to consider. Purchases and sales by the investment companies may provide still more names for consideration.

Another prolific source of ideas can be established by opening a brokerage account—or even suggesting the possibility of doing so. If spending a few dollars is appropriate, there are several investment periodicals that almost always have stock recommendations. Advisory letters can also be purchased—at a variety of prices. Again noting that the decision-making impetus should remain with the investor, these sources should be looked to for ideas but not necessarily for recommendations.

The length of the investor's approved list is a matter of individual choice and relates somewhat to the size of the capital pool. A minimum list of 20 to 25 securities is suggested in order to provide for reasonable diversification.

In selecting those companies making up the approved list, a good deal of attention should be paid to picking representative companies from different industries. The popularity of industries changes from time to time, and the approved list should help the investor respond to such changes. An example in recent years has been the surge in popularity of businesses relating to coal production, which occurred following the shortage and price increase of foreign oil.

Again, the degree of diversification is a function of personal choice and size of the portfolio. Major categories include

- Utilities
- Manufacturing
- Transportation
- Distribution (i.e., retail trade)
- Financial institutions
- Service businesses

If three or four companies were selected in each of these categories, the investor would be assured of representation in a broad segment of the total economy.

The process of becoming informed on the selected companies is much the same as that outlined previously for use with the investment companies. Again, the first step is to write for annual reports and stockholder information. The SEC requires each company to prepare another annual report, called the 10-K report, which is somewhat different from the regular report to stockholders. Although the financial information is necessarily identical, the 10-K report contains more information and is somewhat bulky. Because of the bulk, a special request must usually be made to have it included in the mailing, and most companies will do so.

Study of the annual reports of these types of companies follows essentially the same pattern as that used with the investment companies described above. While these managements are charged with investing in illiquid assets that can only be sold with difficulty, rather than listed stocks with good salability, managers' responsibility to the owners is identical.

Again, the first step in analyzing the report to stockholders (or the 10-K) is to check the auditor's certificate. Qualifications tend to appear more frequently with the noninvestment companies, and the investor is more often faced with a choice between discarding a candidate, ignoring the qualification, or undertaking special analysis. Since the goal is to select 25 or so companies from a list of at least 2500 possibilities, the investor can well afford to be categorical in discarding candidates.

The second step is, again, to read carefully the notes to the financial statements. Some of the principle items that should be noted are discussed briefly in the following paragraphs. Because this is not an accounting book, these comments cannot be fully explanatory, and more detailed information may be needed in specific cases.

Accounts receivable are created when a sale is made, and there rarely is any need for a special note regarding them. If such a note is found, there is a strong suggestion that some unorthodox method of recording revenue is being used, and careful study is indicated.

Inventories are almost always noted, particularly in reference to how cost is determined—by the first-in-first-out (FIFO) method or the last-in-first-out (LIFO) method. When a sale is made, inventory must be reduced by an amount equal to either the price paid for the first piece (FIFO) or by the last piece purchased (LIFO). When prices rise, the first price is generally lower than the last. Since the difference between the sales income and the cost is greater, this makes the profit look good. However, the inventory that was sold has to be replaced at the most recent price if the business is to continue, and this will be reflected against future profits. Hence, more conservative accounting relies on the LIFO method, and businesses are beginning to use it more extensively.

There is almost always a note relating to income taxes. Most companies use one accounting approach to show maximum profit when reporting to stockholders but report lower profits on the tax returns. The taxes must, of course, be paid anyway, so the difference is shown as deferred income tax.

Details of the company's debt are shown in the notes. Particular attention should be paid to the amount of long-term debt which must be repaid yearly, comparing this amount with the net income. If the debt payments absorb all or a substantial portion of the profit, the owners cannot anticipate liberal dividends.

Contingent liabilities generally consist of leases that the business has contracted to pay. These are obligations that are just as binding as a debt, but they do not appear on the balance sheet.

Most companies have a stock option plan that allows its managers to buy stock at a fixed price. The notes show both the number of shares set aside for this purpose and the number of options exercised during the year. In general, exercising the option by actually buying the shares represents a financial commitment by one or more managers, bringing them into a degree of partnership with the owners. The proxy statement will show the actual ownership of shares by the directors and officers.

The purpose of first studying the auditor's certificate and the notes to the financial statements is to determine whether further time should be invested in going through the bulk of the annual report. A good deal of space is usually devoted to describing business activities of the past year, complete with pictures of plants, products, and managers.

There are differing schools of thought on the value of this information. On the one hand, it can be argued that the owners want to know, and should be fully informed, about the business and its future if such a course of action is feasible. On the other hand, the thesis is that the owner can be interested only in the dividend check and the value of his ownership—how the managers produce these results is up to them, except for moral considerations.

Most businesses are going to be doing virtually the same thing next year as they are doing now, and earning about the same amount of money. The exceptions are highly publicized but rare. If a major change in the course of the business is indicated, it is the managers who must recognize it in time to discharge their responsibilities to the owners. Hence, there is some reason to doubt that an investor really needs all the words and pictures in the annual report, and his time may be better spent on other matters.

To analyze the financial statements concisely, a ratio analysis somewhat similar to that used for the investment companies can be used. Calculating the percentage of income before interest and taxes to total assets will indicate how well the managers employed the capital entrusted to them. Relating net income to the sum of common stock and surplus determines how well the owners' equity was employed. The ratio of dividends paid to net income indicates how willing and able the directors are to distribute profits to the owners.

For illustration purposes, we show below the application of these ratios to the 1975 results achieved by IBM:

1. Income before interest and taxes $ 3,423,000,000
   Total assets   15,530,000,000

   Ratio   22%

2. Net income $ 1,990,000,000
   Stockholders' equity   11,416,000,000

   Ratio   17%

3. Dividends paid $ 969,000,000
   Net income   1,990,000,000

   Ratio   49%

One element of major interest to investors is the growth of the business, which is difficult to assess. In an expanding and inflationary economy, almost all businesses tend to show regular growth in reported profits. The key, then, must be to identify those companies growing at a faster rate than the average.

One technique for measuring relative growth is to trace the percentage relationship of the subject company's earnings to one or another of the published averages. Dow-Jones & Company publishes average earnings for groups of companies in the industrial, transportation, and utility industries. Standard & Poor's Corporation also publishes earnings and financial data on some 500 companies in numerous industry groups.

With the information thus obtained, it is possible to compute the ratio of earnings to the appropriate average at various points in time. For example, IBM earned $7.13 per share in 1970 and $14.03 for the 12 months ended March 31, 1976. The 30 Dow-Jones Industrials earned, on average, $51.02 per share in 1970 and $81.87 for the 12 months ended March 31, 1976. IBM was equivalent to 14% of the average in 1970 and 17% in the 12 months ended March 31, 1976; thus, its earnings more than kept pace with this particular group of companies.

It is both possible and practical to make various other tests of the financial data supplied in an annual report, many more than can be discussed here. There are texts on security analysis which describe such calculations, and many of these are published by the investment advisory letters. Those cited above, however, provide a quick and reasonably accurate method of determining the effectiveness of management and some degree of probability that their efforts will benefit the owners. A more detailed analysis appears to be impractical for the nonprofessional investor because of limitations of time and acquired skills, but such an investor need not fly totally blind.

The hoped-for end result of the process described in this chapter is that the investor will have accumulated the capital and skills necessary to embark on a direct portfolio management program, as described in the next chapter. The funds to be used for this purpose will have been segregated and some understanding gained about how investment companies manage their portfolios. An approved list will have been developed of 20–25 companies from which an initial portfolio can be developed.

Although we consider direct investing more desirable generally, contrasted with owning investment company shares, and also believe that portfolios can be managed successfully by nonprofessionals, it is clearly not the only alternative. Some investors who may not have the time or inclination to work at an investing business will be content to invest indirectly. Others may prefer to mix their employment of capital, particularly while testing their skills. The first rule about making money through investments is to avoid losing it; hence investors should exercise maximum prudence in selecting one of these alternatives.

CHAPTER SIX

Benchmark Management for a Quality Portfolio

Investing in common stocks, as compared, for example, with investing in bonds, is a high-risk undertaking. This is not to say that it should be avoided but rather that it must be entered into with caution and with careful attention to some basic rules. The situation might be compared with the use of an electric saw, which clearly has the potential to be very harmful. Many fairly unskilled weekend carpenters have, however, learned to use such a saw constructively, simply by having a great deal of respect for it and keeping in mind some simple safety rules.

The first basic rule about investing in common stocks is that funds should not be used for this purpose if there is a reasonable likelihood that they will have to be withdrawn and used for other purposes. Admittedly, it is not entirely practical to say that any specific portion of one's financial resources will never be needed for emergency purposes. Nonetheless, as we have mentioned previously, unless these funds are sequestered, it is not possible to control the timing of investment actions. If investment decisions are to be based on noninvestment conditions, there is little purpose in trying to manage the portfolio. Thus it is important to have a sizable emergency cash fund before embarking on a common stock investment program.

It might be noted in passing that there is no stigma attached to avoiding the stock market altogether. If one lacks the emotional balance needed to deal with high-risk securities, he is far better off not buying common stocks. Subtle pressures exist in a capitalistic economy that seem to say that everyone should own a share of American industry. The validity, or lack thereof, of that statement is not pertinent to the discussion of investment management concepts; from the manager's viewpoint, such pressures must be ignored. A common stock can only be considered a commodity for making money—if it cannot meet that test, it merits no further attention.

The second basic rule is almost a corollary of the first—do not borrow money to invest in common stocks. The reason is also similar to rule one; a result of borrowing money is diminished control over investment decisions. Furthermore, although it is rarely possible to lose 100% of a common stock investment, the use of borrowed money makes a total loss easily achievable. Many business executives borrowed to exercise options during the 1968–1969 bull market, only to find that the market values disappeared but the debt didn't. Instead, it had to be repaid 100% on the dollar from after-tax savings.

Another way of losing everything on a common stock investment is to sell stock that isn't owned—selling short, in trade terms. This, too, should be avoided, as the risk of a 100% loss largely nullifies any possible gain.

A final cautionary rule is to emphasize diversification, even to the point of deferring a common stock investment program until three or four different issues can be bought. This is important because investing involves probabilities rather than certainties, and there is an undue risk in putting all of the available capital in a single issue. It is far more prudent to keep fairly small amounts invested in individual stocks until the portfolio contains perhaps 12–15 issues. Since no one has found a way to invest money he has already lost, the first goal of any investment program must always be to preserve capital by emphasizing quality and diversification.

With these general rules firmly in mind, it is appropriate to begin creating a management system, the first step of which is to establish specific objectives. There is an old truism which states that you can't get where you're going unless you know where it is. The importance of setting objectives in the management of investments is like most other human activities. The more specific the objectives are, the more probable is success in achieving them.

As pointed out in the preceding chapter, it is vital that there be more than one objective. There is little point in arranging a meeting along Interstate 80 unless some other dimension can be included. There can be no focus to an activity that has only one objective. The objectives must outline the area wherein judgment can be applied by the manager and thereby affect the result.

It is equally important that the objectives be defined in such specific terms that measurement of progress is possible. Numbers lend themselves best to defining objectives of this type. A portfolio manager whose assigned goal is defined as a 5% yield knows very specifically what is expected of him, in sharp contrast to a manager who is told that his objective is "growth" or "stability." Not only is the manager poorly informed, but his supervisor (or client) has no way of monitoring results.

The investment business is one major industry that has successfully evaded the development of modern MBO techniques. Characteristically, managers are simply assigned the broad objective of "capital appreciation" because management fees are based on apparent market values. In a rising market prices go up; the manager looks like a winner, and management fees go up, too. In a falling market, of course, the process reverses itself, except that the percentage charged by the manager goes up.

The basic weakness in a system using the single objective of capital appreciation is that the manager has no influence on the results. During a rising market a diversified portfolio must almost inevitably increase in apparent market value whether the manager shows up for work or stays at home. No evidence has yet appeared indicating that a managed, diversified portfolio increases more (or decreases less) in market value than a randomly selected, diversified portfolio.

Despite the inadequacy of "capital appreciation" as a management objective, it has been the industry standard for well over a decade. Needless to say, one hoped-for result of common stock investing is capital growth; however, that hope does not meet the requirements of a management objective. It is not precise, nor can it be controlled by the manager.

Another important requirement of an effective management system is flexibility, so that objectives can be modified from time to time without impairing the system. Corporate managements may have a return on investment goal of, say, 20% in normal years but can reduce that to 15% during a recession. As conditions improve, a normal rate can be reinstated. It is not necessary to scrap the system (or the manager) to accommodate changes in objectives.

This is equally important to investment managers, as investors' objectives can be quite different and can change from time to time. A young businessman probably has a different objective than does a widow, although both should be free to select an objective. Fifteen years later, however, the businessman may have to change his objective as he faces college expenses for his children.

One objective that meets these requirements for a management system is investment yield. This is the ratio of investment income to capital employed, expressed as a percentage. Such an objective is obviously numerical and precise; it can be controlled by the manager, and it can be monitored. Furthermore, and this, too, is important, it can be determined simply and cheaply.

As discussed previously, investment quality (defined as a proven ability to earn and pay dividends) also meets the requirements for a system objective. The Benchmark measurement system is numerical; others can be made numerical by converting the letter categories into numbers (A+ = 9, A = 8, etc.). The Benchmark system with 99 quality categories certainly provides for precision. Finally, investment quality, like yield, is controllable by the manager and can be monitored. Depending on the system employed, calculation costs vary but are modest.

Application of the Benchmark quality/yield management system is demonstrated in the following discussion, using a hypothetical portfolio. For purposes of this illustration, the preliminary objectives to be used are a Benchmark quality rating of 6500 and a yield of 4%.

Note that these objectives, and the system to be discussed, refer specifically to a common stock portfolio. This is not to suggest that investments should be made only in common stocks, nor that systematic management is not equally effective for managing portfolios made up of bonds or other securities. What is sought is an example that can clearly illustrate the principles and concepts of the system, which then can be applied to other portfolios.

The emphasis throughout is on the total portfolio, not on individual stocks. What we are saying, in effect, is that a common stock portfolio constitutes an enterprise that should be managed in a business-like manner to produce predictable results. While it is to be hoped that the ultimate result of applying this management is to increase the market value of the "business," no manager can be assured that such a development will actually occur.

Even though the ultimate realization from the business may be obscure, whether the business is portfolio management or operating a department store, the manager (or adviser) should be measured by and rewarded for his ability to achieve specific and realistic objectives. Compensation based on the inventory investment in common stocks is a common practice for portfolio managers but would be regarded with horror by a department store chain.

The possibility of realizing on the sale of all or a substantial portion of the business is in the nature of a windfall gain which cannot be anticipated or forecast. The systematic management approach keeps open the option of realizing on windfall opportunities when they do arise by treating such windfall gains simply for what they are. The major thrust of the system, however, is to provide rational management for the portion of the business that is not of a windfall nature. Those who look on windfall profits as normal court disaster.

As a management objective, the 6500 level for quality seems reasonably suitable for a large number of investors, since it stands about two-thirds of the way up on the scale of 100–9900. The exact quality level is a matter of choice by the owner and may be changed from time to time to reflect current needs and the changing economic outlook.

It will be readily deduced that if all portfolio managers seek the maximum quality level, yield among those stocks will tend to diminish as prices rise. Hence what needs to be sought is a balance between quality and yield at a point that most nearly approximates the goals of the owner.

Using numerical measurements of quality allows the graphic portrayal of assigned objectives, a device that is impossible with alphabetic measurements. The objective of a 6500 quality and 4% yield can thus be depicted as a coordinate, 6500/4, as shown in Figure 6.1.

Since the individual stocks that might be purchased for the portfolio also have quality/yield coordinates, it would be theoretically possible to chart some 3000 issues on the basis of their coordinates. If this were actually done, lines drawn through the portfolio coordinate would automatically divide the universe of available stocks into four categories:

1. Low yield, high quality.
2. High yield, high quality.
3. Low yield, low quality.
4. High yield, low quality.

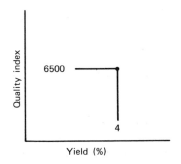

Figure 6-1. Quality/yield coordinate.

The assigned objective coordinate thus serves as a benchmark for determining the suitability of a stock for inclusion in the portfolio. Those stocks to the left of the coordinate in Figure 6.1 are too high in price—and therefore low in yield—to meet the portfolio objective; those to the right are attractive. Issues below the assigned quality level are below the accepted standard and should be avoided.

Over a period of time the thrust of the management system is to encourage the purchase of stocks when they are on the right side of the chart; passing the objective is a signal to sell. Movement from right to left is caused by a rise in the market price.

Since the portfolio objective appears in Figure 6.1 as a dot, a very small price change could shift the stock from the "buy" side to the "sell" side. To avoid a multitude of buy and sell signals arising from minor price changes, it is more practical to set up tolerances for both the vertical (quality) and horizontal (yield) lines.

The tolerance to be set for the quality axis should be fairly small, to the degree permitted by the overall size of the portfolio. The intent is to limit the reflection of price movements to the horizontal axis, rather than to force the manager to balance two factors. On the Benchmark scale, there are about 30 companies represented by each index number. Thus a small portfolio of, say, 5 issues could be limited to index number 65 and still allow a choice from among 30 issues. At the opposite extreme, a very large portfolio might require as many as 10 index numbers but presumably could command the management resources needed to monitor them effectively.

For illustration purposes, we will allow a tolerance of three quality index numbers, 64–66, to support the 6500 objective. The portfolio measurement is obtained by averaging the weighted market value (market value multiplied by index number) for each of the issues. The result is multiplied by 100 to avoid confusing the portfolio index (four digits) with the individual issue index (two digits). Calculator programs for speeding up these calculations are given in Appendix A.

A wider tolerance of plus or minus 10% is suitable for the yield. In order for a stock to move across this range, the price must increase at least 22% above the purchase level. Thus a capital gain of 22% is assured by setting the tolerance at 10%. If the stock is acquired well to the right of the coordinate, the gain will, of course, be larger by the time a sale is signaled. The result of setting tolerances is to give the Benchmark a rectangular form, as shown in Figure 6.2. With the objectives set, the next question is, what resources are available to the management that may produce the desired outcome and meet the objectives? Such resources are common stocks, since we are concerned with managing a common stock portfolio, but there are many thou-

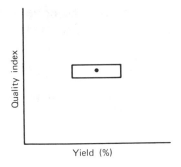

Figure 6-2. Quality/yield tolerance.

sands of common stocks available in the market. Some selectivity has to be shown in developing a list that can be worked with in a practical sense. Known as the "approved list" in most portfolio management situations, it consists of those stocks that the manager has decided are appropriate to the purposes of the portfolio.

The approved list is akin in many respects to the shopping lists that consumers make up in advance of doing their grocery shopping. Knowing the family's tastes and needs for nutrition, the consumer goes to the store with a good understanding of the many products that will suffice to meet these needs. Depending on availability and prices, the consumer will compile the final list of products. For various reasons that cannot be controlled, products will vary in popularity and price during various times of the year, and the consumer will modify the shopping list as indicated by those changes.

The approved list for common stock portfolio management serves a somewhat similar function. A broad list is drawn up of stocks that will tend to serve the portfolio's overall objectives. This list is then drawn upon from time to time, the individual selection depending on prices of the moment.

The approved list must be developed with a considerable amount of care and study. The merchandising apparatus of the securities industry produces an unending flow of suggestions for stocks to be put on approved lists, but obviously not all such candidates can or should be included.

Ideally, no company stock should be put on the approved list until the manager has thoroughly analyzed the business and carefully determined its earnings potential. Unfortunately, there are only a few thousand people in the entire country capable of doing this, and few investors have the time needed to learn and apply the necessary analytical techniques. Furthermore, it is simply not practical for everyone who proposes to invest money in a corporation's stock to meet the management, inspect the facilities, review the financial statements with its auditors, and so forth. Nonetheless, these steps are all essential to careful analysis and stock selection. Lacking such possibilities, the only significant indication that can be used in a practical sense by the average investor is the company's actual performance in the past, which is translated into an investment quality ranking.

Although developing an approved list is a difficult project, it is an essential and important one. The purpose of having the list prepared in advance is primarily to avoid making panicky decisions and hasty analyses at the last minute.

To provide the manager with an ample number of options, the approved list should be reasonably long. Major institutions, for example, will often have as many as 200 stocks on their approved list, even though they rarely invest in more than 80 or 90 stocks at any one time. Thus, there may be two or three alternatives available for each of the stocks currently in a portfolio, each of which has already been screened before inclusion on the list.

For use in the present illustration, Table 6.1 lists 50 stocks that we will treat as the approved list. In compiling this list, we have empha-

TABLE 6.1   APPROVED LIST OF 50 COMPANIES

Company	Quality Index	Yield (%)
1. Aluminum Co. of America (Alcoa)	39	3.5
2. American Cyanamid Co.	80	6.0
3. American Express Co.	68	2.2
4. American Greetings Inc.	28	2.8
5. American Home Products Inc.	97	2.8
6. American Tel & Tel Co.	73	6.7
7. ARA Services Inc.	71	2.2
8. Atlantic Richfield Oil Co.	54	2.8
9. Beatrice Foods, Inc.	63	3.2
10. Bethlehem Steel Corp.	46	4.5
11. Bristol Myers Inc.	92	2.6
12. Burroughs Corporation	31	.7
13. Caterpillar Tractor Co.	78	2.9
14. Commonwealth Edison Co.	88	7.6
15. Continental Can Co.	66	6.3

TABLE 6.1   (*Continued*)

	Company	Quality Index	Yield (%)
16.	Continental Oil Co.	65	3.3
17.	Dow Chemical Company	79	1.7
18.	Du Pont de Nemours Co.	88	3.4
19.	Eastman Kodak Co.	87	1.9
20.	Exxon Corp.	86	5.6
21.	Federated Dept. Stores	65	2.4
22.	General Electric Co.	87	3.5
23.	General Motors Corp.	94	4.2
24.	General Tel. & Electronics	81	7.1
25.	Gillette Co.	94	4.5
26.	Goodyear Tire & Rubber Co.	46	5.1
27.	W. R. Grace Co.	65	6.9
28.	Halliburton Co.	64	.9
29.	Hershey Foods	88	5.4
30.	Household Finance Corp.	61	6.9
31.	International Business Machines	78	3.1
32.	International Harvester Corp.	63	7.6
33.	International Tel. & Tel.	75	7.1
34.	S.S. Kresge Co.	42	.7
35.	Lilly (Eli) Co.	86	2.1
36.	Manufacturers Hanover Corp.	66	6.2
37.	Merck & Co.	93	2.0
38.	Minnesota Mining & Mfg. Co.	83	2.4
39.	Owens-Illinois	41	3.3
40.	J. C. Penney Co.	73	2.3
41.	Phillips Petroleum Corp.	70	2.9
42.	R. J. Reynolds Industries	87	5.0
43.	Sears Roebuck & Co.	68	2.9
44.	Standard Oil (Indiana)	57	4.7
45.	Texaco Inc.	84	8.6
46.	Union Carbide Corp.	77	3.9
47.	U.S. Gypsum Co.	86	9.6
48.	U.S. Steel Corp.	50	4.3
49.	Warner-Lambert	88	2.5
50.	Xerox Corp.	78	2.0

sized names that are probably familiar to most potential investors. We have, in effect, given preference to familiarity and popularity. We do not mean to suggest that this particular list is suitable for any given portfolio. Our intent is to focus attention on the operation of a management system, rather than to try to explain individual stocks.

The fact that a stock is listed in this manner means that the manager is willing to use any one of the stocks in this list. A portfolio will be made up of stocks selected from this list, and from time to time changes will be indicated. The decision to make such changes will be predicated essentially on the quality rating and yield of the individual stocks; other factors of suitability are considered as being equal. When this condition changes, the issue should be deleted and replaced.

The word "use" is employed in this context for a specific purpose. To portfolio managers, stocks must be considered only as contributors to the specified objectives assigned to the manager. He then is in the position of selecting and "using" the stocks that meet his needs, in much the same manner as a chef selects spices and uses them in a blend that meets the taste he has decided on. It is important to avoid attachment to or obsession with any one stock and to judge its suitability strictly on the basis of usefulness.

As noted above, there are literally thousands of stocks from which an approved list can be developed. But business conditions change, business corporations change, and portfolio objectives change. All such changes call for a regular review of the approved list to make sure that it contains at all times a worthwhile selection of stocks for meeting the portfolio objectives.

A more extensive listing of stocks with Benchmark Index Numbers is found in Appendix B, and readers can develop their own approved lists as they see fit. It should be noted, however, that these index numbers are based on 1975 data and may no longer be relevant. Hence a verification of the current index number should precede development of the approved list.

In order to simplify the illustration of how the system operates, we will concentrate on only a few issues and will accordingly rely on a short list of approved stocks. Noting again the objective of 6500 for the portfolio, we will limit the approved list to the 11 issues having an index number in the 60s, as in Table 6.2. A portfolio manager with a 5500 target would similarly concentrate on stocks in the 50s. With the objective already plotted in Figure 6.2 and the coordinates of the issues shown in Table 6.2, it would be simple enough to chart the 11 stocks to show their suitability. However, since only five of the stocks were suitable at December 31, 1975—the date used in the il-

TABLE 6.2   APPROVED LIST OF 11 COMPANIES

Coordinates of Issues as of December 31, 1975

Company	Quality	Yield (%)
American Express	68	2.2
Beatrice Foods	63	3.2
Continental Can (Now "Group")	66	6.3
Continental Oil	65	3.3
Federated Dept. Stores	65	2.4
W. R. Grace	65	6.9
Halliburton	64	0.9
Household Finance	61	6.9
International Harvester	63	7.6
Manufacturers Hanover	66	6.2
Sears Roebuck	68	2.9

lustration—we will assume the investment of $10,000 in each of these issues on December 31, 1975. The portfolio coordinates are then calculated as shown in Table 6.3.

We can now chart the objective, the true (actual) status of the portfolio, and the location of each issue, as shown in Figure 6.3. For visual clarity, the vertical range is 6000–6900, rather than the full range of 100–9900.

The chart shows graphically that, on the whole, the portfolio is in reasonably good condition and that the manager is coming close to meeting the objective. The "actual" portfolio status is somewhat low in quality and clearly is being pulled down by the investment in Household Finance (3). If necessary, the distortion could be corrected by shifting half of the investment in (3) to Hanover (5) or Continental (1), both of which are at 66.

In actual practice, there would be no difficulty in maintaining the quality level because candidates could be picked from among 90 issues rather than 11.

The graphic presentation is an important aid to the decision-making process, since it clearly shows the actual status, identifies the cause for distortion, and indicates the proper corrective action. When funds

TABLE 6.3   PORTFOLIO INDEX FOR THE CHOSEN ISSUES

	Company	Coordinates	Weighted Quality	Income
(1)	Continental	66/6.3	660,000	$ 630
(2)	Grace	65/6.9	650,000	690
(3)	Household	61/6.9	610,000	690
(4)	Harvester	63/7.6	630,000	760
(5)	Hanover	66/6.2	660,000	620
	Total		3,210,000	$3,390
	Portfolio Index		6420	6.8%

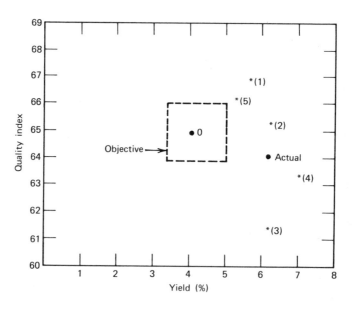

Figure 6-3. Objective, actual status of portfolio, and location of each issue.

are being managed as a fiduciary, the chart should be retained as a permanent record of the decision-making process.

With a computer, it is feasible to test a variety of possible transactions on a "what if" basis, showing the results both numerically and on a chart. In Appendix A there is a program for a programmable calculator that can make the numerical calculations, although it cannot display them graphically.

Portfolio management, like all business management, is a continuing activity, and a key responsibility for the manager is responding to price changes. The chart shows the portfolio status at a given point in time—December 31, 1975, in this instance—but that status must be reviewed from time to time to insure that the objectives are being met. Such reviews might take place daily, weekly, or monthly in the case of highly skilled professionals. For this illustration, we will use a quarterly span, taking another "picture" of the portfolio at March 31, 1976, as shown in Table 6.4. This was an excellent quarter in the stock market, and a 17% gain shouldn't be looked at as typical. It is evident from Table 6.4, however, that this small portfolio participated fully in the market advance.

To assess the impact of those price changes on the portfolio, it is necessary to recalculate the portfolio coordinates and compare them with the objective. The yield ($3390 divided by $58,400) works out to 5.8%, having declined inversely with the 17% price increase, but it still exceeds the target. The quality calculation given in Table 6.5 shows that the 17% increase in prices (overall) has lowered the yield commensurately but has not changed the quality index to any significant degree. This situation arises because the price increases were spread about evenly among the individual index numbers.

TABLE 6.4   STATUS OF PORTFOLIO AT MARCH 31, 1976

	Company	Cost	Market Price	Gain (%)
(1)	Continental	$10,000	$10,200	2
(3)	Grace	10,000	12,100	21
(3)	Household	10,000	12,000	20
(4)	Harvester	10,000	11,900	19
(5)	Hanover	10,000	12,200	22
	Total	$50,000	$58,400	17

TABLE 6.5   PORTFOLIO QUALITY INDEX AT MARCH 31, 1976

	Company	Market Price	Quality Index	Weighted Quality
(1)	Continental	$10,200	66	673,200
(2)	Grace	12,100	65	766,500
(3)	Household	12,000	61	732,000
(4)	Harvester	11,900	63	749,700
(5)	Hanover	12,200	66	805,200
	Total	$58,400		3,746,600
	Portfolio Index			6415[a]

[a] $3,746,600 \div 58,400 = 64.15 \times 100 = 6415$

If there were one or two so-called "hot" stocks in the portfolio, ones that moved very rapidly during the period in question, the impact on the quality index would be greater than shown. If the fast-moving stock were high in quality, relative to the portfolio average, the index would tend to move upward. If it were lower on the scale, then the quality index would tend to come down. Such an eventuality is more probable than the one shown during this particular period; it is rare when the market moves up so consistently, as it did during this particular quarter.

Because the quality/yield coordinate reflects current market price, each recalculation is likely to shift the actual portfolio coordinates. The portfolio Benchmark Index reflects a weighted average, and a change in market price usually changes the portfolio quality (not the quality rating of the individual stock). As shown in Figure 6.4, the pointer at 6500 reflects portfolio quality based on market prices at a

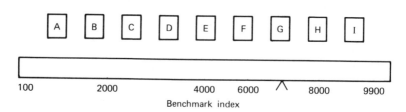

Figure 6-4. Portfolio Benchmark index.

given date. If stock I increases in market value, the pointer moves to the right. Alternatively, if stock A increases in price, the pointer moves to the left. In either event, the move signals the fact that the portfolio is no longer meeting its objective, and the manager is called on to respond to the changed market environment.

A similar illustration can be drawn for the yield calculation, showing that yield declines as prices rise and improves when prices go down. Figure 6.5, the chart of the portfolio at March 31, 1976, thus shows little change from the year-end one.

The basic rule for making stock market gains says to buy low and sell high. Using a numerical quality/yield objective defines the point that separates "high" from "low" in terms of each portfolio's goal. This does not mean that the intrinsic value of the stock has changed, only that the current supply-demand relationship in the market makes it attractive or unattractive for a given portfolio.

The market price for a given stock will fluctuate from time to time for reasons unconnected with quality or yield and often for reasons that apparently no one really understands. Such fluctuations may create an identifiable buying opportunity or a worthwhile selling opportunity. The "ideal" stock for the model portfolio shown previously has a quality index of 6500 and a yield of 4%. If the price goes up, the yield goes down, and it no longer meets the objective. Conversely, a

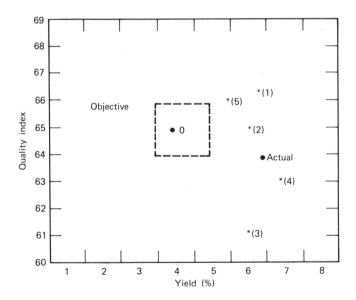

Figure 6-5. Portfolio coordinate reflecting effects of price rises on yields.

drop in price increases the yield and makes the stock more attractive to own since the quality measurement remains constant.

It is apparent from the chart that the five issues still are on the "buy" side of the target zone. A sell signal has, therefore, not yet been given. That occurs when the issue's coordinate moves from the right side of the benchmark to the left side. None of the stocks did this during the quarter, despite the 17% price increase, although they all moved closer to the objective. The distortion caused by Household (3) continues to be evident.

One benefit of setting the 10% tolerance limit on yield, as noted earlier, is to assure a 22% gain before a sell signal is recorded. If the shares are bought at a point far to the right of the objective, an even larger gain is achieved. Thus if Harvester (4) is bought at a 7.6% yield and sold at 3.6%, the gain is actually 111% on the original investment.

Before anticipating gains of such magnitude, it is well to consider the probability that the price will indeed rise that substantially. One way to test this thesis is to check the range in yield during a prior period, such as the year 1975, as shown in Table 6.6. Inasmuch as the sell signal for this portfolio has been set at 3.6%, the table indicates that only Continental (1) would have been a sell candidate in 1975. Thus the portfolio is basically made up of income stocks, and the likelihood of capital gains does not appear promising. If capital gains are important, the approved list should be scanned for more volatile issues and possibly expanded to include some.

Another alternative would be to shift the yield objective further to the right, thus producing a sell signal at a lower price and higher yield.

TABLE 6.6   RANGE IN YIELD DURING 1975

Company	Yield at High Price (%)	Yield at Low Price (%)
(1) Continental	3.4	4.4
(2) Grace	5.7	7.5
(3) Household	5.9	9.3
(4) Harvester	5.6	8.8
(5) Hanover	4.6	7.4

The objective should be more or less constantly under review to keep it consistent with economic trends.

The rule of thumb is that stocks are attractive if the yield is 2% less than that available on long-term bonds. Clearly, if the bond yield changes from 8 to 9%, the objective for the portfolio should be adjusted. For the present portfolio, then, a 6% objective might be appropriate. This would encourage purchases at 6.6% or higher yields and indicate a sale at 5.4%.

Although some portfolios may indeed be oriented to produce income, there is almost always some desire for capital gains. The question then becomes one of determining how aggressively stocks should be sold. Most of the conventional wisdom recommends deferring capital gains but taking losses quickly. This has the benefit of getting the adviser's mistakes out of sight quickly and may indeed be a desirable course of action if the manager is unable to come up with consistent gains. If, however, the manager is able to record gains, even modest ones, on a consistent basis, the best long-term results are achieved by taking gains quickly and reinvesting the proceeds.

Assume the purchase of a stock paying a $4 dividend at 65; the yield then is about 6%. Using the 10% tolerance limit, the stock would be marked for sale at a price of 80, gaining 22%. Table 6.7 shows the investment return if capital gains become available and are taken at the end of the 3 years. It is clear from the table that the average return is greatly reduced by deferring capital gains. That course of action can be justified only if the manager or adviser is unable consistently to replace the issues that are sold with other issues performing similarly.

The purpose of quality/yield management is to focus the manager's decision making on issues that truly can be bought low and sold

TABLE 6.7   INVESTMENT RETURNS IF CAPITAL GAINS ARE TAKEN AT END OF 3 YEARS

	Investment Return (%)			Average Return (%)
Year	Income	Gain	Total	
1	6	22	28	28
2	12	22	34	17
3	18	22	40	13

high. Using the tabular and graphic representations made possible by numerical measuring investment quality, the quality/yield management system does indeed focus the manager's judgment on clearly visible alternatives and also measures the effects of actions taken. Both the goals and the results can be clearly communicated, even to investors or beneficiaries with little knowledge of the investment process.

CHAPTER SEVEN

Benchmark Management for a Growth Portfolio

The term "growth stock" has been so badly overworked by the investment community that it is necessary to provide a definition before beginning a discussion. In the context of dual-objective portfolio management, the following definition will apply:

> A growth stock is one that either (a) shows an upward trend in its quality index, or (b) maintains its position in the top quality category.

Recalling the definition of investment quality as a proven ability to earn and pay dividends, an increase in that ability is good evidence of growth. Hence, any company that displaces one or more companies in the quality ranking must be growing more rapidly. The exception would be those companies at the very top of the list that can maintain that position only by matching or surpassing the best of the other companies. So long as the measurement system is objectively applied to all of the companies, this approach provides a very specific test for identifying growth stocks.

Using this definition, a portfolio made up predominantly of growth stocks could have an overall index of quality at almost any point on the quality scale. A 6500 portfolio would be quite different from a 3500 portfolio, but each could consist largely of growth stocks. The techniques of managing two such portfolios must, however, be quite different, owing primarily to a wider selection of stocks in the higher quality category.

When managing toward a 6500 objective, there is rarely any reason to pass up an opportunity to take a profit. There are many worthwhile investment candidates that rank in this area, most of which have been well researched and constitute a reasonably well-known commodity. It is a simple matter, therefore, to take a profit, pay the tax, and switch to an alternative or even buy back the stock at an appropriate time.

On the other hand, stock selection for a portfolio having, for example, a 3500 objective is much more demanding. Companies found in these lower quality categories tend to be one of three distinct types. One is the young but excellent business that is entering a stage of rapid growth after a faltering start. A second is the so-called turn-around company that is about to recover from a period of trouble. A third type is a company that has never achieved even average success and probably never will.

The hazards of random selection among such a group are obvious. Any commitment of funds to such stocks must be preceded by a thorough analysis, much more thorough than the one needed for a company that has already proven its ability to earn and pay dividends. Close and critical surveillance after making an investment is equally essential.

Because this type of investment management is extremely demanding, it is generally not advisable for part-time investors to attempt it. The skills needed to be successful are those of a top-grade business analyst; further, a considerable amount of study time is required. Nonprofessional investors rarely have the time and skills needed. For this reason, if they want to invest in low-quality stocks, it is usually wiser to seek an investment company specializing in this area.

In planning a management system for a growth stock portfolio, the same measurement tools (quality and yield) can be employed, but the strategy to be employed is different. The calculation of the portfolio quality index, which acts as a fulcrum for the system, involves two variables. One is a change in market values that "tips the scale" so as to push the portfolio index up or down. The other is a change in the quality ranking of each of the portfolio stocks; presumably, this will occur more often and more drastically with growth stocks.

The previous chapter dealt with management of a portfolio concentrated in stocks of above average quality that can be presumed to hold a fairly stable position in the quality ranking. In such a system, the market value variable tends to be the dominant force, and the system as described is geared to respond to changes in market value. Such changes in quality rankings as might occur are generally modest enough so that special attention to them is not necessary.

A management system for growth stocks, by contrast, has to focus more heavily on the second variable, changes in the quality rankings of the various issues. One reason is that the goal of a growth portfolio has to be much longer in term than for a quality portfolio. Because of this longer term and also because growth stocks are of unknown quality until they mature, market popularity is likely to be even more erratic than for the seasoned securities. Finally, the ability to take a profit and substitute an equal quality issue is more limited for low-quality stocks.

Because quality ranking is comparative for all the companies ranked, issues will tend to move up in the ranking as they demonstrate an above-average ability to earn and pay dividends. Companies unable to maintain a regular dividend policy will tend to appear in the lower quality categories. As they mature and begin paying dividends, they too will move up in rank. Over a term of several years, such changes can be sizable.

Not all changes, of course, are upward in quality. A slippage in quality ranking would signal the need for a careful review; however, it is important to keep in mind that the goals are long term and that immature companies can be quite vulnerable to economic adversity. Hence, a good deal of patience may be called for when working with growth stocks.

There probably is no "typical" growth pattern for businesses, particularly in terms of time, but the growth cycle seems to have three major phases.

1. The first phase is the early stage of growth, during which the business is being developed. This is a period of nominal and erratic profits, and basically all profits have to be reinvested either through higher expenses (hence, no profits) or by withholding dividends from the owners. In some instances, this can be a very long phase of the cycle, particularly when a new technology is involved.

2. The second—and most exhilarating—phase is one of rapid growth as the market vacuum is filled and the business potential is realized. Early in this phase it is still necessary to withhold dividends to build financial resources, but in time the owners can look for a share in the profits.

3. The mature phase is usually one of slower growth in percentage terms. Because capital needs begin to lessen, a more liberal dividend policy is feasible, this tends to strengthen the quality index.

The earnings and dividend history of Xerox Corporation over the past two decades provides a worthwhile illustration of these three phases in the growth cycle. Xerox was a successful company even prior to this period, with a long history of success in making photographic papers, but the complete change in its business after World War II resulted in a pattern similar to that of a new venture.

The change that took place at Xerox was a result of its total commitment in the late 1940s to the technology that has since become famous as Xerography. What was then the Haloid Company elected to commit its earning power, financial resources, and management skills to the development and exploitation of this technology. The result was a happy one, and Xerox has come to be one of the major corporations in the nation.

Figure 7.1 traces the earnings and dividend payments for Xerox for the years 1955 through 1975. The top line shows earnings per share, adjusted to reflect the current capitalization, and the lower line shows adjusted dividends per share.

In order to portray graphically the percentage changes in these numbers, they have been charted on semilogarithmic paper. Using this device, it can be readily seen that the decline of $1.07 in per share

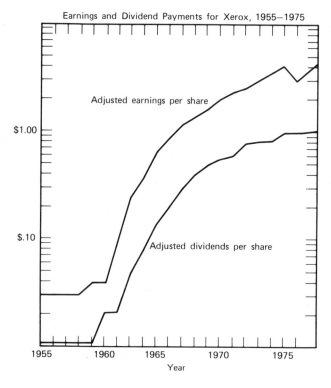

Figure 7-1. Earnings and dividend payments for Xerox, 1955–1975.

earnings during 1975 was a significant but tolerable decline for Xerox; however, had a $1.00 decline in profits per share occurred during the 1960s, it would have been catastrophic. The use of semilogarithmic charting helps keep visible the proportions represented by such changes.

The early phase of growth for Xerox occurred largely before 1960. During the 1950s, it was reporting virtually nominal earnings (based on present capitalization) of $.03–$.04 per share. It should be emphasized that, in this particular instance, the low level of earnings represented a conscious decision on the part of management to underwrite the cost of developing a new business. Most new ventures report poor earnings by necessity, not by choice, since they lack an earnings base to absorb research costs. Xerox's earnings base even permitted the payment of a dividend of a penny per share.

The second phase of the growth cycle, when rapid growth takes place, approximately covered the decade of the 1960s. Earnings per share amounted to only $.04 in 1960 but, at the end of the decade, were in excess of $2.00. This 50-fold increase represents an investor's dream, and few companies can match the Xerox record in consistency and amount. However, even a more modest rate of increase would qualify as a period of rapid growth.

It is easy to visualize the impact of such a period on the company's quality ranking. In each of these years Xerox would undoubtedly have moved up in rank—if the quality ranking system had been used. How far it would have risen would have depended not only on its own performance but the extent of its performance in relation to the other companies in the ranking.

In evaluating the growth of a new-product company like Xerox it is difficult to determine the willingness of the market to buy at a profitable price. Market research can sometimes be helpful, but prior studies indicated that Xerox would fail and that Ford's Edsel would succeed. Thus, only by offering the product at whatever expense may be involved can the extent of the market be determined.

Once adequate demand is found, it is management's responsibility to maintain a worthwhile separation between income and outgo. Since everyone but the government is faced with the same task, it is generally possible to find people capable of doing this. The success of the managers in doing so produces the profits from which dividends can be paid.

A second difficulty is determining when a growth company will reach the point of financial maturity that permits the payment of dividends. Again, prior studies may estimate the need for capital, sometimes with considerable accuracy, but the managers will not distribute dividends to the owners until funds are available for that purpose. Sometimes, a very lengthy period is needed; MacDonald's needed 21 years and 18 billion hamburgers before deciding that it could begin paying dividends. Meanwhile, the market value of its shares had grown to some $2.5 billion.

The challenge in analyzing a growth stock such as Xerox is determining when the growth trend is truly confirmed. It is clearly best to make this determination as early as possible in the cycle so as to obtain maximum benefit from the subsequent growth. Making such a determination, however, is far from easy as year-to-year growth in a small company can be quite erratic. The year-to-year percentage increases for Xerox earnings during the 1960s are illustrated in Table 7.1. Percentage gains become more difficult to achieve as companies grow. The small base in early years results in a large percentage gain from a fairly modest profit. Thus, the increases in per share earnings exceeded 100% in 1961 and 1962 but then dropped to 62% and 74% in the next succeeding years. Keeping in mind that an annual growth rate of 15% will double the size of a business in only a 5-year period, a 60–70% growth has to be considered remarkable, even though it is far less than 100+%. The difficulty in appraising the growth rate lies in comparing percentages, which tend to decline almost inevitably, even though growth is actually occurring at a satisfactory rate.

In retrospect, it can be seen that Xerox was experiencing rapid growth as long as its year-to-year percentage increase exceeded 15%. When that level of growth was reached, the curve began to flatten out into the third phase—one of continuing but more modest growth. Transition into such a stage is not automatic, and some companies slip instead into a decline or a cycle of nominal growth. The test again

TABLE 7.1   XEROX EARNINGS, 1961–1970

Year	Percent	Year	Percent
1961	125	1966	30
1962	167	1967	18
1963	62	1968	18
1964	74	1969	24
1965	35	1970	15

is the quality rank; if this begins to decline, it is clear that the growth period is completed.

Because the Benchmark rankings are still quite new, it is not possible at this time to track the long-term trend of individual stocks. Instead, the system can be implemented by compiling a carefully chosen "approved list" of stocks that have generally been rated in the growth category. Over a period of time, as more Benchmark data become available, the list can be modified as needed.

The mechanics of managing a growth-oriented portfolio are essentially the same as those set forth in the preceding chapter. In order to demonstrate the management process, we will go through an exercise for a growth portfolio similar to the one that was done earlier for a quality portfolio.

Step one in managing a growth-oriented portfolio is, as before, to define objectives and establish tolerances. Nearly every book written about investments emphasizes the need to set objectives for a portfolio, so the concept is far from new. However, most such objectives are expressed in terms such as "capital appreciation" or "income," as opposed to the numerical objectives used in Benchmark investing. The advantage of using numerical objectives, as can easily be seen, is that they are unequivocal, cannot be misunderstood, and can be displayed graphically.

Keeping in mind that the purpose of the growth portfolio is investing in stocks that will improve in quality, it is logical to set the objective at a fairly low point on the quality scale. Ample opportunity is thus provided for upward movement. This is not to suggest that there are no growth stocks in the higher index categories but the possibility for long-range improvement is necessarily less for an issue in the 80s, say, than for one in the 40s.

The ideal candidate for a growth portfolio is a stock that has a fairly low quality rating, either because of immaturity or short-term profit problems, which is about to enter an earnings upsurge. By definition, dividends are not critical to the growth stock investor, but it is anticipated that some dividend increases will accompany the profit improvement. The dividend payments indicate a comfortable balance sheet position, as well as a willingness to share profits with the owners. It is hoped that the institutions will not "discover" the stock and drive the price up to unrealistic levels. If they do, sell.

For illustration purposes, we will use a quality objective of 4000 and a yield of 3%. It should be reiterated, however, that the level can be 5000 just as easily and that inexperienced investors probably would be well advised to start at a higher level.

In setting the tolerances, consideration has to be given to the special nature of a growth portfolio. For the yield, a spread of about plus or minus 10% continues to be reasonable. However, when the 10% is applied to a 3% yield, the spread is quite narrow—2.7% to 3.3%. Hence, it seems more practical to allow a spread of 2.5% to 3.5%, which is plus or minus 17%. A price increase of about 35% would be called for to produce a sell signal. This is in keeping with the growth concept.

Since it is intended that investments will be made in stocks that will improve in quality, the vertical tolerance needs to be sizable. With the quality portfolio, the effort was to concentrate on a horizontal movement; here, we are more interested in a vertical shift. Thus, a tolerance of about 10 index points, say 3500 to 4500, is appropriate.

The quality/yield objective can now be charted, as shown in Figure 7.2. Having set the objectives, the next preparatory step is the development of an approved list. A screening process is involved that is similar to the one used for the quality portfolio, but different factors are emphasized. Consistency in profits and dividends should not be sought, inasmuch as the position on the quality scale indicates that there is none—or very little. More emphasis has to be placed on factors such as market position, product uniqueness, and financial strength—factors that relate more to the future outlook than to the company's proven ability to earn profits and pay dividends. An illustrative approved list is shown in Table 7.2.

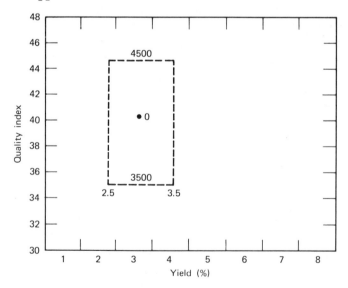

Figure 7-2. The quality/yield objective.

TABLE 7.2   APPROVED LIST OF 50 COMPANIES

	Company	Quality Index	Yield
1.	Addison Wesley Publishing	37	5.5%
2.	Allied Maintenance	44	5.9
3.	American Greetings Corp.	28	2.8
4.	Anderson Clayton & Co.	36	3.4
5.	Arizona Colorado Land & Cattle	28	2.1
6.	Automated Building Components	21	—
7.	Avery Products Corp.	42	1.1
8.	Becton Dickinson & Co.	44	1.3
9.	Bausch & Lomb	39	1.9
10.	Butler International	26	6.3
11.	Chemetron Corp.	37	4.4
12.	Communication Properties	39	—
13.	Data 100	10	—
14.	Denny's Inc.	48	1.6
15.	Digital Equipment Corp.	45	—
16.	Emery Industries	31	4.6
17.	Ennis Business Forms	36	7.6
18.	Faberge	46	7.3
19.	Fairchild Camera & Instrument	35	2.1
20.	Fisher Foods Inc.	43	3.8
21.	Fotomat Corp.	10	0.5
22.	General Binding Corp.	28	0.8
23.	Green Giant Company	39	6.9
24.	Hewlett Packard	35	0.3
25.	Hunt Chemical	50	2.3
26.	International Mineral & Chemical	37	5.3
27.	International Multifoods	46	6.0
28.	Ipco Hospital Supply	45	—
29.	M C A Inc.	45	2.5
30.	Methode Electronics	17	10.7
31.	Microwave Associates	14	—
32.	Motorola Inc.	29	1.7

TABLE 7.2 (*Continued*)

Company	Quality Index	Yield
33. Ogden Corp.	40	6.6
34. Payless Drug Stores	40	2.1
35. Perkin Elmer Corp.	16	1.5
36. Polaroid Corp.	34	1.0
37. Reichhold Chemicals	43	5.7
38. Research Cottrell	43	0.6
39. Restaurant Associates	32	—
40. Robertshaw Controls	38	5.1
41. Savin Business Machines	19	—
42. Seagram Company	31	3.0
43. Sigma Instruments Inc.	42	1.7
44. Smucker J M Co.	44	4.7
45. Stepan Chemical Co.	30	4.3
46. Texas Instruments	34	1.1
47. Thiokol Corp.	31	5.7
48. Vermont American Corp.	35	2.7
49. Western Publishing	38	6.3
50. Zayre Corp.	21	—

Again, in selecting names for the approved list, shown in Table 7.2 we have not limited our criteria for inclusion simply to growth potentials, as would be done in real practice. All of these companies do appear in the lower rankings of the Benchmark rankings and therefore have ample opportunity to move upward; it will be recalled that this is the definition we are using for growth companies. However, we have also tried to select names that may be meaningful to the nonprofessional investor and, further, have included a variety of industries to demonstrate that growth companies are not necessarily limited to one or a few businesses. Thus, and this point needs continued emphasis, the securities on the approved list in Table 7.2 are not being recommended as investments, nor are we contending that they are truly growth companies. They serve merely to illustrate the operation of the quality/yield management system.

In reviewing this list, it will be seen that two types of companies are represented, one yielding fairly substantial dividend income relative to the cost, and the other paying a nominal amount or no dividend at all. Either type can be representative of possible growth, and a portfolio could be made up of issues entirely in one category or the other. If the decision were made to concentrate in either one of these categories, the 3% yield objective would not be appropriate. If the concentration were to be in the higher yield stocks, it would appear that a yield of 5½–6% would be appropriate while, at the other end of the spectrum, the high-priced, low-yield issues would probably not sustain a yield objective in excess of 1%.

Since the portfolio has already been committed to a 3% yield, it is evident that a blend of these two categories is essential in order to achieve that goal. Thus, we must be prepared to compile a portfolio that has a portion of its funds in the high-yield issues and the balance in the low-yield stocks. The first group will provide current income sufficient to offset the lack of income in the second group. Assuming that the price levels of the low-yield stocks are indeed justified by future prospects, these companies will in time presumably be increasing their earnings, thus providing additional profits from which to pay additional dividends.

With these considerations in mind, the securities listed in Table 7.3 are suggested as a growth portfolio for illustration in this exercise. Again, we will assume a $10,000 investment in each.

It will be seen that all five of these issues are in the high-yield cate-

TABLE 7.3   SUGGESTED GROWTH PORTFOLIO

	Company	Quality/ Yield	Weighted Quality	Income
(1)	Ennis Bus. Forms	36/7.6	360,000	$ 760
(2)	Int. Min. & Chem.	37/5.3	370,000	530
(3)	Ogden Corp.	40/6.6	400,000	660
(4)	Reichhold Chem.	43/5.7	430,000	570
(5)	Western Publ.	38/6.3	380,000	630
	Total		1,940,000	$3,150
	Portfolio coordinates		3880	6.3%

gory. In order to obtain a 3% yield, a similar amount of money would have to be invested in stocks with no yield at all. Since that process would basically involve a separate portfolio, this discussion will be limited to the above issues. Using two illustrative portfolios would be more cumbersome and confusing than informative.

Since historical Benchmark data have not yet been published, it is not feasible to show the quality trend of these issues. As an alternative, we have prepared Table 7.4 showing 1971 and 1975 earnings per share and comparing them on an index basis.

By way of perspective, note that the Fortune 500 list of the largest corporations shows a 7% long-term growth rate. Translated into the indexing used in Table 7.4, this works out to 131 in column three. Thus, there is reason to believe that these issues would indeed be moving up in the quality rankings when compared with all of the other companies.

The location of the individual issues and the actual status of the portfolio is shown in Figure 7.3. If the low-yield component of the portfolio were displayed on the same chart, these issues would appear on the left of the target zone. Their inclusion would then pull the Actual coordinate into the objective area.

One difficulty in managing the low-yield portfolio is that there is no way of charting the sell signal. Since all of these issues are already on the sell side of the objective, crossing the zone is not possible. An alternative approach is to use the same percentage gain needed to cross from buy to sell—in this instance 35%—as the capital gain target even though it cannot be shown graphically.

Looking to the five issues in Table 7.4, it is appropriate to review the range in yields that have been recorded in the recent past. Since growth portfolios tend to place more emphasis on long-term trends,

TABLE 7.4   COMPARISON OF EARNINGS PER SHARE, 1971 AND 1975

Company	1971	1975	1975 ÷ 1971
Ennis	$ .06 D	$1.08	Inf.
I M C	.73	9.91	1357
Ogden	1.30	4.62	355
Reichhold	.54	2.32	430
Western	1.55	2.48	160

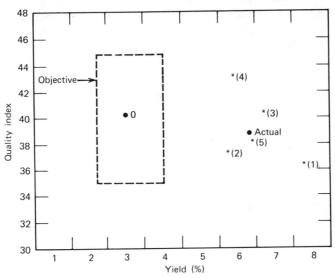

Figure 7-3. Location of individual issues and actual status of the portfolio.

we have made these calculations in Table 7.5 on a 2-year price range, rather than the single year used in the preceding chapter. Again, it can be pointed out that these ranges in yield can be displayed graphically on a chart, as well as listed in a table.

It is apparent from Table 7.5 that in 1974–1975 none of the issues sold at a price high enough to generate a sell signal on the chart. All

TABLE 7.5   RANGE IN YIELDS, 1974–1975

	Company	Yield at High Price (%)	Yield at Low Price (%)
(1)	Ennis	4.6	7.8
(3)	I M C	4.1	6.5
(3)	Ogden	4.7	8.7
(4)	Reichhold	3.9	9.0
(5)	Western	4.9	9.2

of them, however, show a differential of at least 35% between the high and the low, so that use of that target would have produced an opportunity to realize a gain if the stock were purchased in the lower part of the range.

As was the case with the quality portfolio, these issues participated in the general market increase that took place during the first quarter of 1976. The portfolio on the whole increased about 35% in apparent market value. The status at March 31, 1976, is shown in Table 7.6. The new portfolio coordinates are 3878 and 4.7%. Thus, the reinvestment added about 11% to the income stream generated by the portfolio and brought the quality level very close to target.

Again, the quality level was basically unchanged. The large increase in Ennis stock was offset by a modest increase in IMC; the balance was evenly distributed.

The 62% increase by Ennis substantially exceeded the 35% capital gain target, constituting a sell signal. In scanning the approved list for a replacement, Green Giant appears to be a reasonable candidate (39/6.9). Assuming that Green Giant proved to be appropriate, and that the $16,170 received for Ennis were so invested, the new portfolio would appear as shown in Figure 7.4.

It will be noted that three other issues are quite close to the 35% capital gains target. Consideration might therefore be given to realizing these gains as well, reinvesting the proceeds in higher-yielding stocks.

The total investment return obtained during this calendar quarter, using this hypothetical portfolio, consisted of a yield in the amount of 1.6% and a gain of 62%. If the other three issues were also sold, the gain would be 43%. These gains are far above realistic expectations

TABLE 7.6

	Company	Market	Income
(1)	Ennis	$16,170	$ 760
(2)	IMC	10,192	530
(3)	Ogden	13,469	660
(4)	Reichhold	13,571	570
(5)	Western	14,000	630
		$67,402	$3,150
	Portfolio coordinates	3878	4.7%

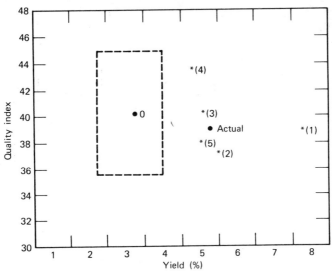

Figure 7-4. Change in portfolio status.

and simply reflect the unusual market conditions prevailing early in 1976.

Again, it should be emphasized that the foregoing exercise is intended to illustrate the manner in which a growth portfolio can be managed under the quality/yield system and that no recommendations are being made as to specific transactions. The purpose is to demonstrate that by setting balanced objectives of quality and yield, the system tends to force the manager to appraise his options in a business-like manner and to reach decisions based primarily upon their impact on the objectives. While it would be pleasant to buy only those stocks that rise in price, such a course is rarely practical, and the rational alternative is to manage the portfolio so as to reach objectives that are indeed achievable, even in the hazy world of growth stock investing.

CHAPTER EIGHT

The Discipline of Selling

A fact not always understood by the nonprofessional investor is that the securities industry is a tremendous merchandising mechanism that has as its purpose the sale of securities to the consuming public. Although in recent years the public has transferred much of its investment decision-making to institutional investors such as pension funds and investment companies, the money still originates with the consumer. Thus, the merchandising mechanism has been modified to accommodate the change in decision-making, but the basic purpose is unchanged.

Most merchandising activities are geared to the sale of products of a tangible nature, rather than the intangible values represented by a common stock certificate. But the basic purposes and functions tend to be quite similar. Most security sales take place in round lots of 100 shares each; at an average price of $50 per share, such a transaction involves the payment of approximately $5000. This figure is probably not too far removed from the average price of an automobile, and there is, of course, a tremendous merchandising effort involved in the automotive industry.

There are other similarities beside the transaction price in the merchandising activities of these two industries. In both instances, the buyers generally lack any real understanding of the products involved and are faced with a bewildering assortment of choices. Lacking the time to become familiar with all of the products to the degree needed to make an intelligent choice, the buyers must rely on advice from someone who supposedly has such familiarity. In most cases, this is the salesman or broker, who is paid a commission only if he succeeds in making a sale, a condition that can sometimes affect his ability to provide objective advice. Both industries invest heavily in advertising that emphasizes reliability and honesty.

Despite these similarities, there are major differences in the merchandising effects of the automotive industry as compared with the common stock market. Purchasing a common stock entitles the investor to a stream of income from dividends, or at least the prospect of such dividends, while purchase of an automobile commits the buyer to a stream of expenses. Further, while the automobile declines in value the moment it is driven off the showroom floor, the price of the acquired stock will fluctuate either up or down; hence, there is at least a 50-50 chance of some increase in value for the investment.

Both automotive marketing and securities marketing represent huge amounts of economic power. If the car business sells 10 million autos during a year at an average price of $5000, the total marketing value is in the area of $50 billion. The securities business, assuming 260 trading days at 20 million shares each day and an average price of $50 per share, represents something in the neighborhood of $260 billion of marketing volume.

It is readily apparent that these huge amounts of money represent tremendous selling power that in turn is used to create a demand for automobiles and for securities. The significant difference between these two activities, for purposes of this discussion, is the fact that automotive marketing is geared to increase the supply of product at a fixed price, while the securities business is committed instead to a fairly fixed supply of product with the price being allowed to fluctuate freely.

Looking first at the automotive transaction, the demand created by the marketing organization is intended to sell as many automobiles as practical, and the factories are run extra hours if necessary in order to meet that demand. The price, at least for a selling year or so, tends to be fairly fixed, and the force of the demand is absorbed at the production level by increasing or decreasing the supply of automobiles.

In fact, the automobile industry has been able to maintain a fairly fixed price over a period of time, when the actual impact of the price is considered. The visible and cutting edge of prices for automobiles is really the monthly payment made by the buyer in financing the automobile. This in turn is a function of the length of time allowed for payment. By increasing the time payment period from 2 to 5 years over a period of time, the industry has in effect been able to keep the visible price of an automobile fairly constant despite inflationary increases in metal and labor costs, as well as rising interest rates. By doing so, the demand created by the marketing mechanism has generally been translated into higher unit sales for the automobile producers.

The common stock market operates in a strongly contrasting manner, tending to work with a fairly limited supply of product and allowing price changes to absorb the impact of variations in demand. While the economic purpose of the stock market is to increase the supply of stock by making possible new offerings of securities in order to raise funds for industry, the fact is that new offerings as such represent a fairly modest proportion of the total common stock market activity. New offerings of common stock, for example, in an active year might approximate $10 billion, obviously a modest proportion of the $260 billion previously noted.

The difference between these two economic effects can be illustrated using some data for General Motors Corporation, one of the leading automobile producers. General Motors had a common stock capitalization in 1975 of 287 million shares of common stock. Translated into round lot transactions, and using the year-end price of $57 per share, the supply of General Motors common stock represented 2,876,430 round lots (100 shares) of common stock. This number remained constant throughout the year, except for some minor exercises of options, but the demand for these round lots was sufficiently strong that the price rose from $31 per share to $57.

Looking at the automobile side of the business, it is apparent that any demand sufficiently strong to justify an 84% increase in prices would have been absorbed instead by an increase in production. The manufacturing schedule would have been revised so that the demand could be met, but the price would have stayed more or less constant throughout the selling.

Recognition of the fact that the securities business is a huge marketing organization dedicated to the creation of demand for common stocks is essential to any systematic approach to managing a common stock portfolio. The fact that the demand thus created translates directly into price fluctuations, owing to the limited supply of product, is of equal importance. Granted these conditions, it then becomes important to determine how the demand thus created is allocated among individual issues, since the impact of that demand will determine the market price for the individual issue.

As with any merchandising activity, the demand for common stock is created by the activity of people whose job it is to sell the stocks to the public. Like most of us, these people are motivated to do their job by the compensation they are paid. It therefore follows that the nature of that compensation program is significant in the way they allocate their efforts.

Again reflecting the simple fact that the securities business is a merchandising operation, compensation to the brokers and advisers is essentially on a commission basis. On each common stock transaction, a brokerage house receives either a commission or a profit, and a portion of that commission—probably 30–40%—is paid to the broker who initiated the transaction. In the case of investment advisers who manage pension funds and investment companies, compensation again takes the form of a percentage based on the apparent market value of the securities.

Under these circumstances, the broker has no alternative but to concentrate his efforts on whatever stock can be sold. His success lies in understanding what can be most easily sold to each individual customer. Like most of us, the broker has a mortgage to pay and children who need shoes, and the only way he can achieve these goals is to sell securities.

The compensation system places tremendous pressure on the broker to keep the commissions rolling, which he does by creating a demand for securities. This type of selling effort is rarely channeled into any specific security, except in the case of a new offering. When the firm becomes involved in underwriting a new issue of stock, the brokers spend weeks and months preparing their accounts to absorb this offering. In ordinary practice, however, the broker is free to sell any security that he find will move. As a rule, the broker's incentive is to close a sales transaction—any transaction—in order to get the commission, without particular regard to the security involved.

As is inevitable under such circumstances, the creation of demand by the broker is basically a random process, in terms of the individual securities that he chooses to promote. In most instances, he is selling into a knowledge vacuum since the investor rarely has any firsthand knowledge of the security involved. Because there is random choice of effort on the part of the broker and the absence of a counterbalancing purpose coming from the investor, the creation of demand for individual stocks is basically a random process. Since the creation of that demand, as pointed out above, translates directly into a price impact owing to the supply limitation, the prices of common stocks also reflect a random process.

The random nature of common stock pricing has been thoroughly explored by others and documented time and again. In brief, these studies consistently demonstrate that there is no known relationship between the action of today's price for a common stock and the price last week, a year ago, or a year in the future. By the same token, the studies also indicate that a random selection of common stocks will, over a period of time, show essentially the same market price fluctuations as one carefully selected by professionals.

To illustrate this point concretely, assume that a stock has risen in price from $15 to $20 per share. One broker will insist that the one-third increase in price means that the stock is on a major upward move and that further price increases are inevitable; therefore, the stock should be bought. On the other hand, another broker will argue that the sizable increase means that the next movement has to be downward since the stock was never worth that much in the first place. In effect, these two approaches come together when both investors agree that the market is wrong, for diametrically opposite reasons; a transaction takes place at $20 per share; and the two brokers earn commissions.

Another element of randomness results from the fact that most purchases of a common stock, instigated by a broker's recommenda-tion, are also accompanied by a separate selling transaction. People who invest in common stocks tend to have all of their money working most of the time, and the brokers are anxious to help them do so. Thus, when it becomes important to buy one stock, it is more or less inevi-table that another stock has to be sold in order to provide the funds. The selection of the stock to be sold is also basically a random proc-ess, since the broker, who is managing the transaction, has no partic-ular preference or purpose in deciding which stock will be liquidated.

Most common stock transactions involve trades between people who are already in the market, due to the fact that there is relatively little new money coming into the stock market. The number of indi-vidual investors increased by about 10 million during the 1960s but has been declining since 1970. The mutual funds were for many years quite successful in attracting new money to the stock market, but for the past three years mutual fund owners have been withdrawing their money.

The new money entering the market today is basically coming from the pension and profit sharing funds. For diversification, a sizable proportion of these monies must be invested in bonds and even real estate, rather than common stocks. While these funds gain around $20 billion annually, there is no real way of accurately determining how much actually finds its way into the stock market during a specific period of time. In reference to a volume of $260 billion or so, how-ever, whatever new money does come in can only be modest in impact.

In order to illustrate the randomness of price actions in the stock market, we have gathered some data on companies whose price per-formance during the first quarter of 1976 was at the extreme opposite ends of the spectrum. The first group consists of 10 stocks that more than doubled in price during the first quarter of 1976, while the sec-ond group consists of stocks that declined at least 10% during the same period. Since the first quarter was one of strong market demand and rising prices, these two categories tend to show extremes in market performance.

If any single factor were to be selected as the one that should most probably influence market action, it would be earnings per share of common stock. Unless a company earns profits, it cannot pay dividends. If its profits improve, there would be a rational expectation that the stock price might also improve. Conversely, a worsening of the profit picture would presumably justify some decline in the market price. Thus, we have divided the 10 companies in each of these categories into those showing improved profits, those with decreasing profits, and those showing no significant change in earnings during 1975 as contrasted with 1974.

Table 8.1 shows the profit picture in 1974 and 1975 of those companies that showed at least a 100% increase in market price dur-

TABLE 8.1   PROFIT PICTURE IN 1974 AND 1975 OF THOSE COMPANIES THAT SHOWED A 100% INCREASE IN MARKET PRICE DURING FIRST QUARTER OF 1976

	Earnings per Share	
Change in Profits	*1974*	*1975*
IMPROVED		
Litton Industries	$(1.26)	$ .84
Cubic Corp.	(.49)	1.22
Houston Oil & Mineral	1.37	1.99
Merrill Lynch	1.04	2.69
DECREASED		
Bobbie Brooks	.02	(1.25)
Electronic Memories	.37	(.61)
Singer Corp.	(.89)	(27.68)
Wyly Corp.	(1.86)	(6.27)
NO SIGNIFICANT CHANGE		
Fedders Corp.	(.95)	(1.08)
Kewanee Industries	2.87	2.90

ing the first quarter of 1976. The first four companies in Table 8.1 did show a noteworthy improvement in profits in 1975, in two instances moving from a loss position to a significant profit. Certainly it would be understandable if the shares of these companies increased in price, at least to some extent if not as much as 100%. However, there were also four companies that suffered drastic decreases in profits during the same period but nonetheless had essentially similar market action for the stocks. Finally, the third category shows that Fedders continued to lose money at about the same rate that it had and that Kewanee was continuing to earn money at about the same rate; nonetheless, the shares of both doubled in price in the first quarter of 1976.

Table 8.2 shows the profit picture in 1974 and 1975 of those 10 companies that showed a decline in market price of 10% or more during the first quarter of 1976. Only 3 of the 10 companies in Table 8.2 show the profit decline that supposedly would justify a reduction

TABLE 8.2   PROFIT PICTURE IN 1974 AND 1975 OF 10 COM-
PANIES THAT SHOWED A DECLINE IN MARKET PRICE OF 10%
OR MORE

	Earnings per Share	
Change in Profits	*1974*	*1975*
IMPROVED		
Albertson's Inc.	$1.85	$2.38
Archer-Daniels-Midland	1.19	1.40
Baker International	1.68	3.23
Vetco Offshore Inds.	1.23	2.54
Florida Power	2.42	3.93
DECREASED		
Old Republic Insurance	4.62	(5.41)
Quaker Oats	1.91	1.45
U A L Inc.	4.01	(.24)
NO SIGNIFICANT CHANGE		
Central & Southwest Corp.	1.76	1.72
Marion Laboratories	1.39	1.23

in market price. The other companies either showed significant increases in profits or very modest changes. These 10, however, were the worst performers for this particular period of time.

Systematized management for a common stock portfolio must necessarily be predicated upon rational transactions taking place between a willing and informed buyer and an equally willing and informed seller. Unless such a premise is established, there is no purpose in attempting to manage a common stock portfolio, in the sense of investing time and money on decision-making. In fact, the studies show that a simple random process of stock buying and selling will be equally effective if the trend of market prices is used as the measurement of success.

The question that arises is, "What should the informed decision-maker be informed about?" If his success is being measured by market trends, presumably he must be informed about the future trend of the stock prices for the shares that he plans to purchase. However, all of the evidence says that price trends for common stocks are random, and there is no possibility of being informed about a random condition.

In order, therefore, to manage a portfolio systematically, rational transactions have to be based on some factor other than market performance. The key factor is the *suitability* of a given security to the objectives of the portfolio. The only legal justification for recommending a security for purchase by a consumer is its suitability to his purposes. So long as market prices are random, the possibility of price appreciation cannot be considered an element of suitability.

If price appreciation is eliminated as a measure of suitability, what then can serve as such a measure? We argue herein that the quality/yield correlation can be defined for a common stock portfolio and that this correlation can then serve as a measure of suitability.

Granting that the quality/yield correlation is a determinant of suitability, the fact nonetheless remains that pricing for these shares in the portfolio still reflects random activities. This would imply that the quality/yield portfolio will neither benefit more from the random action of the market nor suffer more heavily than other portfolios. Thus, it might simply be argued that the management system need only be dedicated to selecting stocks on the basis of suitability.

On the other hand, however, having based the need for systematic management on the premise that stock market prices act in a random manner, the system should also be prepared to react to random changes in prices, both on the buying side and on the selling side. In constructing the demonstration portfolios discussed previously, we

104 Quality Controlled Investing

have shown how the manager can respond to market prices that produce attractive and suitable candidates on the basis of the quality/yield
correlation; the second half of the system, however, must also encom-
pass an aggressive selling activity.

It is generally much easier for investors to buy stocks than to sell
them. The merchandising mechanism provides an impetus to buy as a
first priority; the suggestion to sell is made only if new money cannot
be found. A person who is willing to commit a substantial sum of
money to buying shares of stock must have a strong streak of optimism; having made an emotional commitment to the company involved, it is difficult to contemplate the necessity or advisability of selling. One doesn't start talking about divorce at the wedding. Thus,
there is an ingrained tendency simply to ride with the stock unless
some total disaster occurs.

Most advisers and brokers will recommend that the investor continue to hold stocks that improve in market price but to sell losers
rapidly. These recommendations are usually based on expectations of
future market price changes and ignore the proven randomness of
price trends.

The background of these recommendations is quite understandable; advisers and brokers don't want to be reminded of recommendations that resulted in a declining market price, which is what will
happen as long as the stock is on the portfolio list. Naturally, if the
stock price does in fact go up, they can take the credit for what was in
truth a random result.

Since there seems no reasonable likelihood that the random nature
of stock market prices is going to change, prudent management suggests that a systematic approach must be made to selling stocks so as
to lessen their exposure to these random measurements. A number of
selling systems intended to serve this purpose have evolved over the
years and are discussed below.

One of the simplest and most common approaches to systematic
selling is the *stop-loss* order. In essence, this approach suggests that the
buyer can best determine the point at which the stocks should be sold
when he makes the purchase. Thus, he enters an order with the broker
to sell if the price drops two points or 10 points or whatever. As indicated by the title, this procedure is intended to stop a loss in liquidating
value since the order should automatically be executed when the designated price appears in the market.

The other side of the same process would be a *stop-gain* order,
which would cause a selling order to be entered when the stock rises in
price two points or 10 points or whatever. The very words "stop-gain"

are basically repugnant and therefore are never used. The dislike for the phrase, of course, reflects the thought that nobody wants to stop a gain from increasing and, for this same reason, few people actually do undertake to sell at a predetermined price.

The major drawback of any price-based selling system is the fact that it is indeed price-based and is therefore predicated upon the randomness of market prices. It is clearly difficult to make rational judgments in a random market, but the thesis underlying this selling system is that prices will inevitably change and that entering a predetermined order will indeed stop a loss from increasing and will secure any profit that might develop without any further decision-making.

Another system, which also is predicated largely on price actions, is one involving the liquidation of the poorest performers in the portfolio at some regular time interval. Some businesses seek to upgrade their marketing organizations by periodically replacing the lowest 10% of the salesmen in terms of performance; a similar approach can be followed with respect to a common stock portfolio. The drawback is again that the randomness of stock prices makes judgments of this type somewhat questionable.

There are also selling systems that are geared essentially to time periods, rather than price action. One such approach assumes that there is a strong seasonal factor in the pricing of common stocks. The rule of thumb is that stocks should be sold on Good Friday and again just before Labor Day but that they should be purchased near Memorial Day, Fourth of July, and Thanksgiving. Considering the activity that would result from following this approach, one would have to assume that it was initiated by a very hungry broker.

A more rational time-based approach to systematic selling of stocks involves an annual liquidation process. There are variations within this basic approach. One is to liquidate all gains at the end of the year, pay the tax, and set the balance aside, using only the original funds for future investing. This has the advantage of locking in the gains and protecting them from possible dissipation by future price action. A second approach is to realize all the gains but also offset them to the extent necessary with losses. This approach naturally tends to reduce the amount of taxes that would be paid at the time.

The management system described herein introduces still another approach to an aggressive selling system. The essence of managing a portfolio on the basis of a quality/yield correlation means not only that securities are added to the portfolio only when they are suitable to its objectives but also that securities must be sold when they no longer meet its objectives or are destructive of them. The regular calculation of the quality/yield correlation will signal selling opportunities when the random nature of the pricing mechanism destroys the suitability of one or more stocks for a given portfolio. Selling the stock at that point may not be the only or the best solution, but the system does force the issue out for a decision-making process.

In order to illustrate the application of these selling systems, we will trace their use with respect to the quality-oriented portfolio discussed in Chapter 6. Specifically, we will deal with that portfolio as it stood on March 31, 1976—some 3 months after it was structured. The portfolio at that date is shown in Table 8.3.

TABLE 8.3.   PORTFOLIO AT MARCH 31, 1976

		Actual	Target
Quality index		7023	6500
Yield		4.9%	4.0%

Company	Cost	Liquidating Value	Apparent Gain (loss)
A T T	$ 5,087	$ 5,650	$ 563
Beatrice	2,350	2,350	—
Cont. Can	8,250	8,737	487
DuPont	6,325	7,300	975
Kodak	5,306	5,937	631
Exxon	8,875	9,387	512
G E	2,306	2,625	319
Grace	7,350	8,925	1,575
Household	4,800	5,737	937
I B M	11,212	13,100	1,888
Int. Harvester	6,712	7,912	1,200
Phillips	2,706	2,800	94
Stanolind	12,786	14,212	1,426
U. S. Steel	6,500	7,950	1,450
Xerox	2,543	2,781	238
	$93,108	$105,403	$12,295

It is important to emphasize that the following discussion is intended only to illustrate possible uses of various selling systems, not to suggest that these transactions are recommended or implied as being beneficial. A more concrete application of the quality/yield system is set forth in the next chapter.

Looking first to using a stop-loss order, the portfolio happily presents no occasion for such a transaction. If Beatrice is used for illustration purposes, it would be possible to enter an order to sell if the stock declined in price to 18½, or $1850 for the 100 shares. Having been purchased at 23½, a stop-loss order at 18½ would limit the drop in price to around 20% by automatically selling the shares at that price.

There appears to be no guideline or rule of thumb for setting the price on a stop-loss order. Presumably, an investor with little confidence might limit the loss to 10% or even 5%. However, if he feels that insecure, he might be much better off to avoid the stock altogether.

A similar lack of guidelines is noted for a stop-gain approach, but the illustrative portfolio does provide a number of candidates. If the target were set at 20%, three of the issues would already be likely sale candidates:

- W. R. Grace with a 21% gain
- Household Finance with a 20% gain
- U.S. Steel with a 22% gain

If the liquidation target were set at a 15% gain, three other companies would be added to the candidate list:

- DuPont with a 15% gain
- I B M with a 17% gain
- Int. Harvester with a 18% gain

There is a great deal of merit to the argument that the best time to select a selling price for a stock is at the time of purchase. Understanding of the issuing company is probably then at a peak, and an objective judgment as to a reasonable gain is probably practical.

The basic weakness of the approach, in terms of systematic management, lies in the fact that it deals basically with stocks on an individual basis, not with the portfolio as a whole. An automatic sell order removes from the manager the option to balance the strong stock with one less strong, at least momentarily. All we are suggesting is that the option should be kept open; the judgment of each manager determines whether it should be exercised.

TABLE 8.4.   SELL ISSUES, BY "LOW 10" APPROACH

Company	Cost	% of Total	% Gain
Beatrice Foods	$2,350	2.5	—
Phillips Pet.	2,706	2.9	3.0
Cont. Can	8,250	8.4	6.0
Exxon	8,875	9.5	6.0

To return to the football team analogy, there may be times when the halfback can't move the ball, but the fullback can. The automatic decision, whether stop-loss or stop-gain, would call for the removal of one or the other of the running backs even though the team's success depended upon the combination. It is important to recall that the role of systematic management is to improve the application of judgment, not to substitute for it.

The "low 10" approach, if applied to the demonstration portfolio, would indicate the sale of at least two of the four issues in Table 8.4. Here again the test of suitability is predicated on market action, and application of the system takes the management initiative away from the manager. The annual liquidation concept can be tested with these data only if we assume that the period covered by the comparison was 12 months rather than 3 months. If that assumption were made, all of the issues except Beatrice Foods would be sold, producing the following results:

Proceeds of sales	$103,053
Cost basis	90,758
Taxable gain	12,295
Less tax at 30%	3,688
	8,607
Add back recovered cost	90,758
Investible cash	$ 99,365

Use of this system would permit the realization of gains and the payment of taxes, still leaving $99,365 for reinvestment. Since the basic purpose is to segregate gains and remove them from risk, however, the $8607 of net gain would be withdrawn from the enterprise, and only the original $90,758 would be available for investment.

There is a degree of attraction to this system in a rising market; particularly if the investor's tax rate is below the maximum for capital gains. Gains are indeed isolated from future risk, and, perhaps more importantly, there is no build-up of a large potential tax burden that might impede sales at an appropriate time in the future. If the tax rate is below the maximum, the system chops up the gains into small enough pieces so as to keep the overall rate at a fairly low level.

The management system described herein is intended to measure selling opportunities on the basis of suitability to the portfolio objectives as expressed in the quality index and the yield. In the specific example, the 7023 quality index was slightly above the target level of 6500. The return based on cost of 4.9% was well above the 4.0% target, and the current yield (based on market prices) of 4.3% also exceeded the goal. Thus, the system would indicate a stand-pat attitude as of March 31, 1976.

Two basic premises underlie the advocacy of an aggressive selling approach to common stock portfolio management. The first of these is that the random nature of price actions in the stock market makes it impossible to forecast with any degree of reliability future trends in stock prices. Nonetheless, it is wholly practical to develop a system that can react to random price actions but aggressive selling is needed to assure a measurable degree of success.

The second important premise is that common stock portfolios are managed in order to produce cash benefits to the owners, and such benefits can be realized only by selling. It is, of course, encouraging to read in the newspaper that stock prices are rising and that a portfolio could possibly have been liquidated yesterday or last week at some handsome amount. Most advisers welcome this concept since they are paid in cash for paper profits. To the owner, however, such profits are meaningless until they have been translated into cash.

CHAPTER NINE

Business Accounting
for Investments

Throughout the preceding discussion, we have sought to emphasize the importance of viewing an investment program in the same way one looks at any other business enterprise. We consider the commitment of hard-earned savings to this purpose to be a decision of considerable importance and one that demands discipline and a businesslike approach. The measure of success for a business, including an investment enterprise, is provided in the records, which show how much money was made available to the business and how successful the managers were in producing additional money.

The goal of any business enterprise is the generation of funds that, at the owner's option, can be allocated to other activities. This is not to say there may not be psychic satisfactions as well in conducting a business enterprise, and these can be meaningful to the owners. Such satisfactions, however, represent the viewpoint of individual owners and may not be applicable to all businesses. The necessity for creating profits, on the other hand, can certainly be presumed to have a universal applicability for business enterprises.

A business comes into existence when an investment is made. Characteristically, such an investment is made in the form of money, but it is also possible to create a business by investing time and talent. For purposes of this discussion, we are assuming that the investment is made in cash under the conditions outlined earlier in this book.

The purpose of the enterprise that we are discussing is to generate cash for the owner. There is often a tendency in looking at an investment enterprise to be satisfied with theoretical market values as an end objective. The existence of unrealized market values, however, is a step toward the objective but cannot be an end in itself. The final step in the investment process is realization of either gain or loss so that the owner truly does have the option of using the cash as he chooses.

As in any business enterprise, it is important to account carefully for all of the monies disbursed by the business, as well as those that are received. An accounting system is ordinarily devised to keep track of these matters, and the organization of that system in itself reflects the purposes of the activity. An accounting system that stops at that point of registering apparent market values for an investment portfolio clearly identifies the creation of apparent market values as the objective of the management system. On the other hand, an accounting system that measures the cash return to the owners as the completion of the cycle puts quite a different demand on the managers.

Although accounting systems have become increasingly complex as businesses themselves have become more complex, the essential fact remains that an accounting system can effectively show only three things:

1. The amount of money put into the business and thereby made available to the managers.
2. The way in which the managers employed the funds made available to them.
3. The return that was achieved by the managers from employing the funds made available to them.

The accounting system devised to measure and disclose these three factors can in itself provide a considerable amount of discipline for the management. If the accounting system emphasizes the wrong objectives, then the management will direct the enterprise toward an erroneous goal. If, for example, all the emphasis in a retail store is on obtaining sales volume, with little regard for expenses, it is highly probable that the business will show a great deal of activity but little or no profit.

A similar situation prevails in conducting an investment enterprise. If the accounting system is set up as to indicate that success has been achieved simply when apparent market values are visible, then the managers certainly are going to concentrate their efforts on creating such apparent values. On the other hand, an accounting system that emphasizes cash receipts and cash payouts to the owners will force the managers into a different pattern of managing.

In this present discussion, our concern will be with the cash inflow and cash payout approach for the accounting of the enterprise. Rising stock prices reported in the paper may provide enjoyable reading, but we do not consider the business to be effective until the owner has money in his pocket. Creation of apparent market values may be likened to a way station, which may be more or less comfortable depending upon circumstances, but the trip is not complete until the money reaches home once again.

It might be noted that this approach is the one most commonly used in business. There is a rule of thumb in almost every business other than investment companies that assets should be valued at the lower of cost or market in order to avoid the display of illusory values. Furthermore, since the accounting system is designed to provide, among other things, some means for measuring the effectiveness of management, the accounting system must restrict itself to those activities that the managers control. These actions are reflected in the purchase of assets at cost, since that decision is the one that management made. Management actions are not shown by reflecting random pricing in a market that the managers cannot influence.

The conventional practice in accounting for investments, in distinct contrast to other businesses, almost always tends to emphasize market values rather than costs. A parallel situation would be for a metal working firm to mark up or mark down the value of its equipment depending upon the level of metal scrap prices. The theory would be that the equipment could be better sold for scrap than used in the business. If scrap prices increased, the manager would feel entitled to a bonus, using the investment industry approach.

In a business sense, common stocks in a portfolio perform the same function as the metal working machinery in the industrial company. The purpose for having a portfolio is to achieve objectives set by the owners; we are assuming that the owner's overall objective is to increase the amount of money he has to spend.

The accounting system proposed here has purposely been kept simple and consists essentially of two reports. The first is a cash receipts and disbursement table that shows, for a given period of time, the cycling of cash through the investment process. The second is a portfolio status report that details the composition of portfolio assets at a given point in time. Taken together, these documents answer the three essential questions posed above:

1. How much capital was available?
2. How was it used?
3. What were the results?

The form suggested for the cash receipts and disbursements report is shown in Table 9.1. (A detailed illustration to fill in the blanks will be shown later.) Table 9.1 is intended to show only the major types of receipts and disbursements that are to be expected in an investment enterprise, but the list of items can be expanded if necessary. The use of a yearly period is conventional, but a shorter period is also feasible. The final column, showing a total for the three periods, is not truly essential and becomes both awkward and less valuable as the number of periods increases. It is included primarily to show the possibility and technique of preparing a multiyear report.

It will be seen that the ending cash balance for one period becomes the beginning cash balance of the next. This results from the assumption, made for this illustration, that all the funds generated by the business will be retained and reinvested. If the owner chooses to

TABLE 9.1   FORM FOR CASH RECEIPTS AND DISBURSEMENTS

	1973	1974	1975	Total
BEGINNING CASH BALANCE				
RECEIPTS				
Dividends				
Capital gains				
Sale of securities				
Savings				
Other				
Total				
DISBURSEMENTS				
Purchase of securities				
Commissions and charges				
Taxes on income				
Taxes on gains				
Other				
Total				
ENDING CASH BALANCE				

withdraw cash, another item would be added below the disbursements total showing Withdrawals, thus producing a different cash balance that will then become the beginning cash balance. It is this process that gives rise to the concept of cycling cash through a business.

The items listed under Receipts in Table 9.1 need little explanation, but some comment might be appropriate for the disbursements schedule. In this system, separate reporting is made of the actual market price of the securities purchased or sold and the expenses associated with the transaction, such as commissions, transfer taxes, and so on. These latter items represent operating expenses for the business even though, for tax purposes, they are included in the purchase price and deducted from the proceeds of sale. Regardless of tax considerations, these are disbursements that take cash away from the owner. They should therefore be clearly identified and closely monitored, as is true of any expense.

Taxes fall into this same category of expense, despite their inevitability. Since the tax rate for earned income may be different from the rate applicable to capital gains, provision is made for both types. If nothing else, highlighting the amount of tax paid should be important at election time.

The Other disbursements category in Table 9.1 would most likely consist of investment-oriented services and publications used in conducting the business. These can range from the daily newspaper, which contains the essential market price and dividend data, all the way to elaborate and expensive advisory services.

A valuable and efficient publication for even the small investor is the *Security Owner's Stock Guide* published monthly by Standard & Poor's Corporation. This contains, in tabular form, important investment information on more than 5000 common and preferred stocks. It also contains rankings of common stocks that, if translated into numbers, can serve to some extent as quality index numbers. The cost, about $40 for a year's subscription, can be justified even for a small portfolio.

Investment advisory services are numerous and range widely in price. There is no way to describe them or appraise them in a book since they cannot be rated good or bad until someone defines "good" and "bad."

Interpretation of the cash receipts and disbursements report will be discussed subsequently, in relation to an illustrative investment program.

The form of the Portfolio Status Report, the second component of the accounting system, is set forth in Table 9.2. This sample is set up

TABLE 9.2   FORM FOR PORTFOLIO STATUS REPORT

Date _____
Quality objective _____
Yield objective _____

	A	B	C	Total
1. Shares owned				
2. Cost per share				
3. Total cost				
4. Dividend income				
5. Return on investment				
6. Market price				
7. Apparent usable cash				
8. Less charges				
9. Less taxes				
10. Balance				
11. Quality index				
12. Yield				

to show only three securities in the portfolio; actually, there may be many more. In such an event, it would be appropriate to show the items on the horizontal axis and list the securities vertically.

The first three items in Table 9.2 show the amount of money used to assemble the portfolio. Included in Total Cost are the commissions and other charges, which are shown separately in the disbursement schedule. For illustration purposes, we will assume that these amount to 2% of the transaction price. The next two items measure the effectiveness of management in employing capital. Dividend income (line 4) is the amount currently being received. If the stock has been owned for several years, the current dividend may be significantly greater than it was when the purchase was made; nonetheless, the return on investment calculation (line 5) is based upon the actual original cost.

As has been pointed out previously, the return on investment (ROI) test is widely accepted as the best single measurement of management skill, regardless of the type of business. The calculation is quite different from the computation of yield, which is shown in line 12, and serves a completely different purpose. The question being answered by the ROI calculation is How well have the funds been employed? If the owner, who may also be the manager, finds this result consistently inadequate, he should look to alternative investment programs.

It will be noted that the ROI calculation does not include capital gains, whether realized or anticipated. However, if gains are realized and reinvested, the resulting increase in the capital pool means an enhancement for the owner even if the ROI itself remains constant. A business earning 4% on $50,000 of capital is clearly more valuable than one earning 4% on $40,000. It does not necessarily follow that unrealized appreciation of, for example, $10,000 is more valuable than unrealized appreciation of $5000.

The third section of the Portfolio Status Report (lines 6–10) is used to determine the cash available for reinvestment if the portfolio were to be liquidated in whole or in part. Line 7 is the result of multiplying line 6 and line 1. From this amount must be deducted the transaction costs and the tax that must be paid. There is an assumption that the shares can be sold at the listed prices, even though the table has to be based on historical prices, and there can be no guarantee that these prices actually will be realized. Since there is no practical alternative method for obtaining price information, the assumption has to be tolerated.

Lines 11 and 12 serve as a focus for decision-making, the primary use for this schedule. The two tests for suitability, quality and yield, are displayed both for the individual issues and for the portfolio as a whole. The yield calculation is based on current market price, rather than cost, as well as the current dividend.

In analyzing the status report, the effort is directed toward determining how well the portfolio is meeting its assigned objectives. If it is doing so, and if the ROI is satisfactory to the owner, no change is indicated. If an issue is destructive of the portfolio objective, it can be quickly identified as a logical candidate for sale, regardless of its ROI. Quite conceivably, a single issue may show a high ROI (indicating that it was purchased at an attractive price in terms of the objective) but a low yield. The logical decision then is to liquidate the investment and reinvest the proceeds. If the total portfolio ROI is satisfactory, the manager can reach this decision with confidence in his ability to replace the sold investment in such a way as to benefit the enterprise.

In order to illustrate the purpose and use of this accounting system for investment management, we have worked out a three-year investment program using the concepts set forth previously in the chapter on quality investing. The specific steps involved in applying both the management system and the accounting system are described in the following paragraphs.

It should be noted at the outset that we are forced to use quality index numbers of individual securities based on current figures even for historical purposes. We are using the Benchmark Index Numbers noted earlier, which are based on 1975 data. Even though the program that we are outlining presumes an initial investment in 1973, we are forced to use the 1975 quality data because comparable figures were not available for 1973. We do not consider this a major handicap because quality figures do not generally change that drastically in a few years, and the illustration can therefore be used to demonstate the functioning of the system.

Our assumption was that the enterprise would be funded with $5000 in 1973 and that the initial capital would be added to at the rate of $200 per month. The latter figure, of course, presumes a savings program for increasing the common stock investment activity.

With the limited amount of money available, we have assumed that the initial purchase would be of an investment company, for reasons outlined earlier in the book. This step would provide professional management for the funds and also provide diversification that would not otherwise be available for this sum of money.

Thus, the first transaction that we have assumed to have taken place was the purchase of 400 shares of Adams Express Company during 1973 at an average price of $12 per share. The price of Adams ranged from a low of $11 to a high of $14.75 during 1973, and we are using an approximate midpoint of $12 per share for this illustration.

Starting with $5000, the 400 shares of Adams could be bought at $12, representing a total investment of $4800. In addition, such a purchase would entail payment for commissions and other charges. For purposes of this illustration, we are using a 2% charge for commissions and expenses since that appears to be a fairly realistic expectation. Commission rates are no longer identical among firms, and it is possible to find a variety of commissions being charged. Most of them, however, have to be fairly close in amount, and the 2% figure seems reasonable for this example.

Assuming the purchase of 400 shares of Adams on the New York Stock Exchange, the total outlay would come to $4896 including the

2% charge. The initial cash advance, therefore, would be reduced to $104, and by the end of the year $2400 would have been added to that amount.

Incidentally, Adams Express was chosen for this exercise because it is first on the alphabetical list of closed-end investment companies discussed in an earlier section of this book. Its use here is not meant to suggest that it is or is not an appropriate investment for anyone reading this book.

During 1973 the owner of 400 shares of Adams Express common stock would have received two distributions from the company. One was a dividend of investment income of $164. This dividend would be subject to tax, and, using our assumed 30% tax rate, the balance in cash would be $115. The second distribution was $296 of capital gains. Since we cannot know the individual tax structure, we will also apply a 30% tax to this distribution. Adding these receipts to the balance remaining of the original investment of $104 and the savings for the year of $2400, the investor would reach December 31, 1973, with cash available for investment of $2826.

As noted earlier, the selection of Adams Express Company as an investment vehicle in this exercise represented an arbitrary choice and was not necessarily predicated upon its suitability in terms of investment objectives. One of those objectives, the Benchmark Index Number, was 5512 based on 1975 data, and we will have to assume that it was approximately the same in 1973. The yield, on the December 31, 1973, market price, was 3.2%. This quality/yield correlation was in line with the pattern shown previously in Figure 5.1.

Thus at the end of 1973 this hypothetical investment enterprise would have the bulk of its capital invested in a diversified investment company and would also have $2,826 available for some other investment purpose. Rather than suggesting in this illustration that additional funds be put into Adams or some other investment company, we are supposing that the manager would at this point begin a program of direct investing, the first step of which would be to determine an objective for the enterprise. In actual practice, such a decision might be premature, but we will accept it for purposes of illustration.

As the sums of money involved are quite small, we will assume that a good deal of emphasis will be placed by the manager on quality issues. If the sums were larger, a small proportion might be set aside for speculative investing, but at this stage of the process, emphasis should be on quality. Thus we proceed on the assumption that the manager has set up a quality/yield objective of 7000 on the Benchmark quality index scale and 4% on the yield index.

Quality stocks generally were selling at fairly high prices at the end of 1973, and many of the familiar investment names would not have been suitable in terms of these objectives. One candidate that seems appropriate, however, was Stauffer Chemical Company, which has a Benchmark Index Number of 67 and was available at a yield of 4.9% at the end of 1973. The stock was selling at 40¾, and we will assume that the manager of this portfolio bought 50 shares at that price. After paying a 2% commission, the total outlay would have been about $2077.

After this transaction, the assets of the enterprise would be:

Cash	$ 749
Adams Express stock	4896
Stauffer Chemical stock	2077
Total	$7722

Those figures are based on cost rather than market value. The market value of the Stauffer Chemical stock is identical with cost since it is presumed that the transaction was made at the close of business. Adams Express closed 1973 at 12⅝ per share, as contrasted with our assumed average cost price of $12; hence, there would be $250 of unrealized capital appreciation.

During 1974 the investment enterprise would build its cash balance to $3551 by year-end as a result of investment income and savings, as shown in Table 9.3. With this amount of cash on hand, the manager would presumably seek at this point to invest directly in additional securities. The prices of quality issues tended to fall during much of 1974, and a greater selection among high quality issues was available at the year-end. For this exercise, we have assumed that the manager would invest in the purchase of 100 shares of Heublein Inc., then available at 20⅛. Adding 2% expenses, the total investment would use up $2045 of the cash available.

Heublein carries a Benchmark quality index number of 97 and was available on a 5.5% yield at the end of 1974. Thus, its addition to this portfolio would bring the quality level well above the 7000 mark that had been established as an objective. Under the circumstances, the manager might then feel justified in taking a more speculative position in a lower quality issue that showed potential for rapid growth.

In the furtherance of this objective, we will therefore assume that the manager, at the end of 1974, buys 100 shares of Denny's Inc., which carries a Benchmark quality index of 48. Denny's was priced at

TABLE 9.3   CASH RECEIPTS AND DISBURSEMENTS, 1974

BEGINNING CASH		$ 749
RECEIPTS		
Dividend from Adams	$ 184	
Dividend from Stauffer	95	
Capital distribution, Adams	296	
Savings	2400	
Total receipts		2975
TOTAL CASH		$3724
DISBURSEMENTS		
Tax on Adams dividends	$ 145	
Tax on Stauffer dividend	28	
Total disbursements		173
ENDING CASH BALANCE		$3551

6⅝, calling for a total investment of $675 when a 2% charge is added. The yield on Denny's was only 3.0% at December 31, 1974, somewhat below the portfolio goal, but the assumption of rapid growth with a probable increase in the dividend, plus the above average yield on the balance of the portfolio would permit its inclusion.

At the end of 1974, giving effect to these transactions, the enterprise would have its assets distributed as follows:

Cash	$ 824
Investment Company shares	4,896
Direct investments	4,797
Total	$10,517

As noted earlier, the quality index for the Adams Express portfolio was 5512, and a substantial portion of the total was still invested in this vehicle. The three direct investments, treated as a single portfolio, had a quality index number of 7714, well above the goal of 7000. On a combined basis, the quality index was 6669.

Reflecting the then current dividend levels, the return on investment from these investments was 4.3%. On the securities owned directly, the indicated yield based on anticipated dividend pay outs was 4.9%. Thus, the overall yield for the investment enterprise was significantly above the 4% target.

The decline in market prices of many stocks during 1974 also resulted in a decline in the market price for Adams Express Company common stock, which ended the year at 7⅞. This was well below the average of $12 per share that we had assumed as the original cost. Stauffer Chemical Company, on the other hand, showed a modest increase in price, ending the year at 42¾. Thus, there was an indicated capital loss of about $1100 on Adams Express and an indicated gain of $100 on Stauffer, assuming that the investments might be liquidated on December 31, 1974.

During 1975 the enterprise would have built its cash balance to $3616 as a result of dividends received and continued accumulation of savings. This is illustrated in Table 9.4.

While we assume that the manager watched this portfolio carefully during the year 1975, we will make the assumption that he saw

TABLE 9.4   CASH BALANCE, 1975

BEGINNING CASH		$ 824
RECEIPTS		
Dividend from Adams	$ 196	
Dividend from Stauffer	115	
Dividend from Heublein	110	
Dividend from Denny's	28	
Capital gains from Adams	112	
Savings	2400	
Total receipts		2961
TOTAL CASH		$3785
Less taxes at 30%	$ 169	
ENDING CASH BALANCE		$3616

no need to make any changes during the year. To some degree, this is simply an arbitrary assumption made to facilitate the demonstration of record keeping for this illustration, and our reliance on this assumption should not be taken to indicate that no changes should have been made during the year.

The status of the portfolio at the end of 1975 is shown in Table 9.5. It will be seen that we are making two percentage calculations in this recapitulation table, both relating to the dividend income. The first calculation, referred to as Yield, shows the relationship of the 1975 income to the market price at the end of 1975. The second calculation, referred to as Return on Investment (ROI), relates the same dividend income to the cost of the securities, as contrasted with the current market value.

As noted earlier, these two calculations are used to serve two different purposes. In the sense of judging the effectiveness of the management, the return on investment calculation is the more descriptive. In effect, this calculation says that the manager was given $9,693 to work with and that the current rate of return on that investment is 4.6% from current income and 5.8% including actual gains. The yield calculation, on the other hand, serves to test the suitability for continued inclusion in the portfolio of the individual holdings. These yield figures are then contrasted with the yield objective for the portfolio, which, as noted previously, has been set at 4%.

Using this test, the entire portfolio would be susceptible to liquidation since the current yield of 3% is below the assigned goal. All three of the direct investments have risen in price to the extent that they are

TABLE 9.5   PORTFOLIO STATUS AT END OF 1975

	Cost	Market Price	Yield (%)	ROI (%)
Adams	$4,896	$ 4,050	4.8	4.0
Stauffer	2,077	4,250	2.7	5.5
Heublein	2,045	4,675	2.3	5.4
Denny's	675	2,050	1.4	4.1
Total	$9,693	$15,025	3.0	4.6
Including capital gain			3.7%	5.8%

now destructive of the objective, rather than contributing to it. Adams has actually fallen off in price, and the yield accordingly exceeds the 4% target, although the return on investment continues to be at the assigned level.

Under the circumstances, it would be appropriate to evaluate the option of liquidating the entire portfolio and reinvesting the proceeds. As shown in Table 9.6, such a process would make available a total of $16,831 for reinvestment. To review the progress and achievement of the management of this portfolio, it can be pointed out that liquidation at this stage would show a total return for the 3-year period of $4781 on an investment of $12,200. In itself, this represents a total return of 39% over the 3-year period, an average of around 13% per annum. In actual fact, the $7200 of savings was available for only half the period; allowing for this change in the calculation, the overall return is 56%, or almost 19% per annum.

The achievement of a 13% annual return, on the average, for 3 years justifies the conclusion that systematic investment based on quality considerations can indeed produce a satisfactory growth in capital. If this same program were carried through for another 5 years, continuing to average only 13% annually, the initial fund of some $5000 would have reached almost $47,000 at the end of the fifth year. This is illustrated in Table 9.7. The fact that a return of 13% does produce fairly substantial gains when compounded strongly suggests that the systematic manager should be looking for certain and frequent profits,

TABLE 9.6   CASH AVAILABLE FOR REINVESTMENT

Cash on hand		$ 3,616
Sell securities	$15,025	
Less 2% expenses	300	
Total	$14,725	
Cost recovery	9,693	9,693
Gain	$ 5,032	
Less 30% tax	1,510	
Total gain		3,522
Cash available for reinvestment		$16,831

TABLE 9.7   TOTAL CASH AT END OF FIVE YEARS, WITH 13% ANNUAL
RETURN

Year	Cash	13% Annual Return	Savings	Total
1	$17,000	$2210	$2400	$21,610
2	21,610	2809	2400	26,819
3	26,819	3486	2400	32,705
4	32,705	4252	2400	39,357
5	39,357	5116	2400	46,873

even though they may be fairly modest in amount. In other words, it is not necessary to reach for the sky in managing funds in a common stock portfolio since careful selection and realistic selling practices can produce quite satisfactory returns with only modest risk.

As in any management activity it is important to test occasionally the status of the business and plan its future activity. The end of the year is conventionally selected for this purpose, and we will therefore review this current portfolio as of the end of 1975. In doing so, however, we do not mean to suggest that more frequent than annual reviews are inappropriate; to a considerable extent, the value of quarterly or even monthly reviews depends upon the activity within the business. More active portfolios should probably be looked at very carefully every month.

The Portfolio Status Report, one of the two basic schedules in the accounting system, provides a concise recapitulation of essential information about this investment enterprise, which can be used as a review and decision-making document. The report is shown in Table 9.8. As we have pointed out previously, the most effective single test of management performance is the return on investment. In this instance, Table 9.8 shows us that the manager has been provided with funds sufficient to enable him to invest $9693 for securities. The return on these investments, in the aggregate, is $449, resulting in an ROI of 4.6% to the total cost.

It can also be observed from Table 9.8 that the manager has indeed been quite capable of locating and acquiring investments that are productive of the target assigned to the portfolio. At this stage, all four of the investments are producing a return on investment at least equal to the objective of 4%, based on cost.

Table 9.8   Portfolio Status Report

December 31, 1975

| | | Quality objective | | 7000 | |
| | | Yield objective | | 4% | |

		Adams	Stauffer	Heublein	Denny's	Total
1.	Shares owned	400	50	100	100	NA
2.	Cost per share	12	40¾	20⅛	6⅝	NA
3.	Total cost (add 2% charges)	$4896	$2077	$2045	$ 675	$ 9,693
4.	Dividend income	196[a]	115	110	28	449[a]
5.	Return on investment (ROI)[b]	4.0%	5.5%	5.4%	4.1%	4.6%
6.	Market price	10⅛	85	46¾	20½	NA
7.	Apparent usable cash	$4050	$4250	$4675	$2050	$15,025
8.	Less 2% charges	81	85	93	41	300
9.	Less 30% tax on gain[c]	(278)	626	761	400	1,510
10.	Balance	$4247	$3539	$3821	$1609	$13,215
11.	Quality index	5512	67	97	48	7053
12.	Yield[d]	4.8%	2.7%	2.3%	1.4%	3.0%
13.	Cash on hand					$ 3,616

NA–Not applicable.   [a] Excludes capital gains distribution.   [b] Line 4 divided by line 3.   [c] Line 7 minus line 8 minus line 3 times 0.3.   [d] Line 4 divided by line 7.

The second portion of the table (lines 6–10) focuses the attention of the manager on the options open at this date. In sum, this states that a reasonably prompt liquidation program for the portfolio would probably produce something in the neighborhood of $13,215 of cash for reinvestment or other purpose. We have also shown the cash on hand of $3616, taken from the cash receipts and disbursements schedule.

The derivation of the $13,215 can be traced in Table 9.6. The market values for each of the securities at the end of 1975 are listed. Like buying gasoline at a station, the posted price never fully reflects the total cost, and we have made some arbitrary estimates on deductions. These include 2% for commissions and taxes and the 30% tax provision that we have used throughout.

Lines 11–12 in Table 9.8 are used in determining how well the portfolio is currently meeting the assigned targets of a 7000 quality index and a 4% yield. In making this calculation for the total portfolio, the Adams Express index of 5512 has to be reduced to 55.12 in order that it be comparable in a numerical sense to the individual index numbers.

Overall, it can be seen that the portfolio is very much on target in terms of quality, although there is a wide range among the four issues. The clear-cut problem, of course, is in the yield, which is substantially below the assigned target.

It is also clear from Table 9.8 that the four securities then held were destructive of the portfolio objective. Adams was exceeding the objective in terms of yield but fell considerably short of the quality index target. The other three securities were substantially below the yield target at this date although, as shown on line 5, they were well above the target when acquired.

As pointed out previously, the manager at December 31, 1975, had a total of $16,831 of cash available if the decision were made to liquidate this portfolio. Essentially, this sum was made up of some $3616 of cash on hand, plus the recovery of the $9693 of cost, and a gain (net of costs and taxes) of $3522. This sum can be verified by adding line 10 and line 13 on the portfolio status report.

The options available to the manager at this point can be summarized in three categories. First is simply to maintain the status quo, a course of action that is far from reprehensible since line 5 indicates that the portfolio is indeed producing in accordance with the plan—based on actual capital employed. The second option is to modify the portfolio in some way, using the cash on hand to strengthen one of the existing security positions or to add a totally new investment to the group. The third option is to liquidate the portfolio—a decision that the management system proposes—because all of the securities are now destructive of the portfolio objectives.

A fourth alternative may also be briefly noted, namely, to liquidate the portfolio and take whatever profits are forthcoming. Since we are presuming an ongoing business activity, however, we will ignore this possibility, although it should always be actively considered as an option.

In view of the fact that the system, as indicated on line 5, has been performing well for the enterprise, it would indeed seem unreasonable to abandon it at this stage. Therefore, we will assume that the portfolio is liquidated immediately with sufficient promptness so as to obtain actual 1975 year-end prices and to reinvest the available funds also at the 1975 year-end prices. This is not a very likely occurrence, but it can suffice for purposes of illustration.

Assuming, then, that the liquidation has been carried out, the manager now finds himself with almost $17,000 in cash, which he must promptly employ. The approved list set forth in Chapter 6 was developed for just such a purpose, and we will turn to it for investment candidates.

Looking at the approved list (Table 6.1), it will be seen that 21 companies meet the yield test, 12 of which are above the portfolio targets for both quality and yield. These 12 are listed in Table 9.9. In the interests of diversification, it is proposed that some 5 or 6 issues of the 12 be selected for purchase. We will assume that these purchases can be made at the December 31, 1975, market price and that an additional 2% of the purchase price will be needed for commissions and transfer expenses.

It is also suggested that purchases be made on the basis of round lots of 100 shares each. This is generally the most economical way of purchasing stocks. Looking at the above list, and keeping in mind our diversification goal, it would seem appropriate under these conditions to concentrate on shares selling in the 25–30 price area. Using shares with a higher price, such as Exxon, results in an undue concentration in that issue and tends to lessen diversification.

With these conditions in mind, the suggested list for reconstituting a new portfolio at December 31, 1975, is as follows:

- 100 shares of Commonwealth Edison
- 100 shares of General Telephone
- 100 shares of International Telephone
- 100 shares of Texaco
- 200 shares of U.S. Gypsum

TABLE 9.9   APPROVED LIST OF 12 COMPANIES

Company	Quality Index	Yield	Market Price
American Cyanamid	80	6.0%	24⅞
Am Tel & Tel	73	6.7	50⅞
Com. Edison	88	7.6	30¼
Exxon	86	5.6	88¾
G M C	94	4.2	57⅝
G T E	81	7.1	25⅜
Gillette	94	4.5	33⅜
Hershey Fds.	88	5.4	18⅝
I T T	75	7.1	22½
Reynolds Inds.	87	5.0	61½
Texaco	84	8.6	23⅜
U.S. Gypsum	86	9.6	16⅝

It will be observed that in selecting the five companies for the portfolio we have avoided those having a quality/yield position close to that assigned for the portfolio. If such companies were included, a fairly modest change in price levels would presumably make them candidates for sale and call for a restructuring of the portfolio. By concentrating funds in issues that are well above the portfolio standards, minor fluctuations in market price can be absorbed without necessitating a wholesale realignment and redeployment of funds.

Looking at the five selected issues, the quality index works out to 8330 on a portfolio basis, and the yield is 7.8%. Various methods for making these calculations quickly are shown in Appendix A. Purchase of these shares would involve a total outlay of approximately $13,900, including commissions and charges, leaving a cash balance of around $3100.

With a well-diversified, high quality portfolio made up of these five issues, some consideration might be given to incorporating a "growth" issue in the same manner that the Denny's stock was used earlier. A logical candidate on the approved list is American Greetings, Inc., with a quality index of 28 and a yield of 2.8%. The purchase of 300 shares of American Greetings would involve an outlay of approximately $2700. This transaction would bring the total investment up to $16,600, with a quality index of 7431 and an overall yield of 7.0%. Thus such a security could be included and still maintain both the quality standard of 7000 and the yield of 4%. Note that consideration of a nonconforming issue such as this is totally separated from the basic strategy.

An alternative, assuming that the intent was to continue concentration on high-quality issues, would be the purchase of 100 shares of American Cyanamid at a cost of around $2600. If this option were exercised, the quality index would be 8279 and the yield 7.9%.

For purposes of illustration, we will assume that the manager of this investment enterprise elected to balance the high quality issues with 300 shares of American Greetings.

As noted earlier, the basic record of the development of this business is in the cash receipts and disbursements schedule described earlier. Table 9.10 reproduces that schedule, this time showing the actual amounts involved in the hypothetical portfolio.

TABLE 9.10   CASH RECEIPTS AND DISBURSEMENTS

	1973	1974	1975	Total
BEGINNING CASH BALANCE	$5000	$ 749	$ 824	$ 5,000
RECEIPTS				
Dividends	164	279	449	892
Capital gains	296	296	112	704
Savings	2400	2400	2400	7,200
Other	—	—	—	—
Total receipts	$7860	$3724	$3785	$13,796
DISBURSEMENTS				
Stock purchases	$6837	$2675	$ —	$ 9,511
Commissions and charges	136	52	—	189
Taxes on income	49	84	135	268
Taxes on gains	89	89	34	212
Other	—	—	—	—
Total disbursements	$7111	$2900	$ 169	$10,180
ENDING CASH BALANCE	$ 749	$ 824	$3616	$ 3,616

To sum up, then, the program outlined herein would, in three years' time, have brought the investor from a modest initial capital contribution of $5000 to a well-diversified list of six stocks costing $16,500. The indicated return from this portfolio on an annual basis would be $1157. This amount of indicated income would represent 23% of the original $5000, a return of 7% on the $16,600 currently invested and 9.5% of the initial capital plus savings. By March 31, 1976, the apparent liquidating value would have risen to $19,162, an increase of 16%.

CHAPTER TEN

Summing Up

Considering the full spectrum of investment opportunities provided by the markets for corporate securities, there is a tremendous range in investment risk. At one end of the scale are corporate bonds, which fluctuate only modestly in price. At the other extreme are common stocks, which fluctuate widely and unpredictably. In between are debentures and preferred stocks with fluctuations generally less than common stocks but greater than bonds.

The extent of this range can be seen by comparing price movements during the period 1969–1973, when there were very wide fluctuations in stock prices. The Dow Jones Industrials reached a high of 1051.70 in 1973, a point some 67% above its low of 631.16 in 1970. By contrast, the Dow Jones average for 40 bonds was only 17% above its low (reached in 1970), when it set a high for the period of 75.34, also in 1973. Thus, during this particular span of time, common stock prices, as represented by the Dow Jones Industrial Averages, were about four times as volatile as were bond prices. The volatility of lesser known stocks was even greater.

Price volatility can clearly represent a hazard if the investor finds himself buying high and selling low. On the other hand, the same price volatility can provide profit opportunities if the investor can limit himself to buying low and selling high. The key to success therefore lies in locating the measurement that can be used to separate "high" from "low." A management system capable of improving judgment in this area thus offers the possibility of converting these hazards into opportunities.

Another striking difference between the bond market and the common stock market is the use of quality measurements. These are thoroughly integrated into the functioning of the market for bonds but virtually ignored in the stock market. In between again are the pre-ferred stocks, where recognized quality measurements exist but tend to be less influential on decision-making than in the bond market.

The inverse relationship between price volatility and the use of quality measurements cannot be dismissed as coincidence. Simple logic insists that quality measurements are used by bond buyers as the essential criterion that distinguishes a high price from a low one. When the price gets too high for a bond of given quality, the demand disappears and the price cannot rise further. Similarly, when the price is attractively low, buyers become active. Thus, the use of quality measurements provides a correcting mechanism that tends to limit price volatility.

It is clear that no such correcting mechanism plays a significant role in the market for common stocks. Wide fluctuations in stock prices are commonplace. They are rarely understandable even in ret-rospect, and no one yet has demonstrated an ability to predict them. Hence, price changes in the stock market are considered to be ran-dom, rather than rational.

In this stock market environment, successful management must depend on an ability to respond to random price changes. No purpose can be served in trying to forecast any truly random activity, and man-agers are not paid to sit idle and watch fluctuations in price. Whether the manager is also the beneficiary of a common stock portfolio, or simply a professional managing other people's money, he must em-ploy his best judgment in concluding that a stock price is high or low. The quality managed system has been designed to strengthen that judgment-making process.

How does it do so? In the preceding chapters, we have shown in detail how the management system functions. But, to recapitulate, we will briefly review the process. For this illustration, we will assume a quality/yield objective of 6500/4%, using the Benchmark Index Numbers as quality measurements. For an approved list, we will use the 30 companies that are used in calculating the Dow Jones Industrial Average (see Table 4.2).

The simplest way to meet the 6500/4% objective would be to in-vest in a single company having a 65 Benchmark Index Number and yielding at least 4%. No company meeting these specifications is among the 30 issues in Table 4.2. However, 3 are to be found on the approved list in Table 6.1: Continental Oil Company, Federated De-partment Stores, and W. R. Grace Company, all of which have a Benchmark Index Number of 65.

These three issues are plotted in Figure 10.1. Since it is obviously

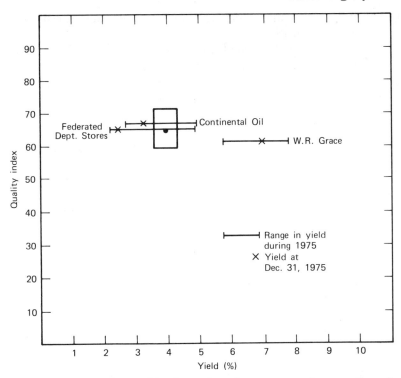

Figure 10-1. Quality/yield chart for three companies meeting the 6500/4% objective at Dec. 31, 1975.

not feasible to place all three issues on the 65 line, we have separated them slightly for visibility. The horizontal line shows the range in yield during 1975, and the small vertical mark indicates the yield at December 31, 1975. Shown in Figure 10.1 is the income of a given quality (65), which could be purchased with $1 in 1975. At the low price for the year, Continental Oil common stock was yielding more than the designated portfolio objective (4% plus or minus 10%) and was therefore suitable for purchase or continued ownership. The same was true of the other two issues; in fact, Grace was a suitable purchase even at its lowest yield.

It will be seen that the yield line for both Continental and Federated crossed the target zone during 1975. Thus, these two issues would have been identified as purchases when yielding over 4.4% but marked for sale at 3.8% yield. In order to make this crossover, the price of the stock had to increase about 22%. Hence, the manager would, by responding to these signals, generate for the period a gain of 22%. The investment period would necessarily be no more than 12 months in this particular illustration.

Charting the quality/yield objective for the portfolio and the quality/yield coordinates for a stock provides a graphically simple management tool. Issues that appear to the right of the objective are suitable for the portfolio; those to the left are not.

The value of a common stock portfolio to the owner or beneficiary is enhanced both by assuring an attractive current return and by generating capital gains. The decision-making that is necessary to achieve these goals is simplified by use of the chart in a quality-managed investment system. In this illustration, stocks would not be purchased unless they provided at least a 4.4% return and would be sold when they had risen at least 22% in price, thus generating a capital gain in that amount.

Returning to the approved list (Table 6.1) 30 Dow Jones Industrial stocks, we must still look for the one stock that comes closest to meeting the 6500/4% target. The most logical candidate is American Can Company, as shown in Figure 10-2. At the end of 1975 American

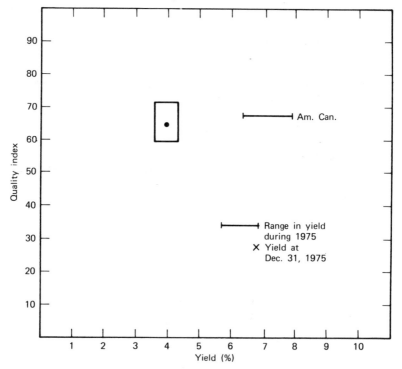

Figure 10-2. Quality/yield range of American Can Co. in 1975.

Can was selling at a 7.0% yield, having traded in a fairly narrow range during the year. It had a Benchmark Index Number of 67; on that basis, it qualified for the portfolio. In the past, the stock has sold at a price high enough to result in a 3.5% yield, at which point it would be a sale candidate. Figure 10.2 shows the range for a single year only; it would be equally feasible to show a 2-year or 3-year range—whatever the manager found most suitable.

While it is generally feasible to find an issue with satisfactory quality/yield coordinates, it is more usual to reach the portfolio target by a blending process involving two or more issues. This option is illustrated in Figure 10.3, which shows similar quality/index data for Sears Roebuck & Co. and for International Harvester Company. If equal investments were made in the two issues, the portfolio quality index would be 6550, versus a 6500 target, and the yield at 5.2% would be well above the 4.0% target. Under these circumstances, the manager might defer the sale of Sears even though it is not suitable in and of itself. That decision might reflect such considerations as the cost

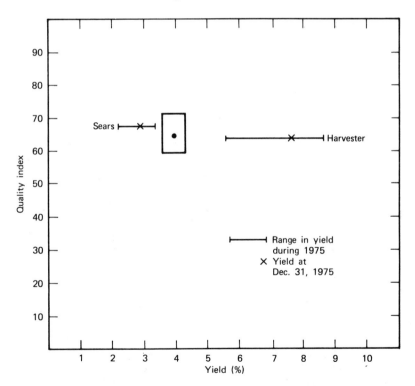

Figure 10-3. Blending process using two issues.

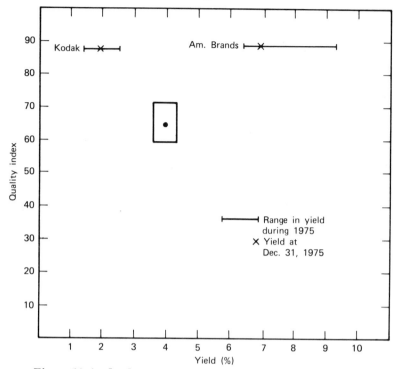

Figure 10-4. Blending issues to meet portfolio yield objectives.

at which Sears had been purchased and the impact of taxes that would become payable if the stock were sold.

Even at very high quality levels, it is possible to blend issues to meet portfolio yield objectives, as shown in Figure 10.4. Here two high-quality issues from the approved list have been blended in equal proportions. Eastman Kodak at 87 and American Brands at 88 are clearly of excellent quality, and on a combined basis they produce a quality index of 8750 and a yield of 4.4%.

A similar process can be followed with issues of lower quality as can be seen in Figure 10-5. Goodyear at 46 and Alcoa at 39 produce an index of 4250, when combined in equal proportions, and a yield of 4.3%. Goodyear shows a particularly wide range in yield, and therefore market price, indicating greater volatility than Alcoa or, for that matter, both Sears and Kodak. A manager emphasizing capital gain potentials might seek out issues with greater volatility in market price.

The result of blending all six of these issues can be seen in Figure 10.6. Such a portfolio would come very close to matching the 6500/

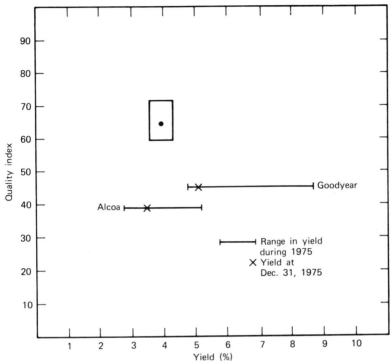

Figure 10-5. Blending issues of lower quality.

4.0% objectives. The quality index would be 6517; the yield, based on December 31, 1976, prices, would be 4.6%.

Parenthetically, it should be noted that continuing efforts should be made to improve the approved list and that such efforts may disclose attractive but overlooked opportunities. For example, a possible substitute for International Paper (73 and 3.5%) might be Belknap, Inc. (also 73 but yielding 9.7%). Belknap has a dividend record going back to 1880, as contrasted with 1946 for International Paper, but has received little attention from the market.

Returning to our six-stock portfolio, the yield would have dropped to 4.2% by March 31, 1976, a logical review date. Contributing to this decline were further yield reductions in Kodak and Sears. Sale of these two issues would rebuild the yield to 5.2% but drop the quality index to 5900. Reinvesting the proceeds in Exxon (86) and General Foods (71) would maintain the 5.2% yield and restore the quality index to 6550.

A management system is meant to assist the manager in his

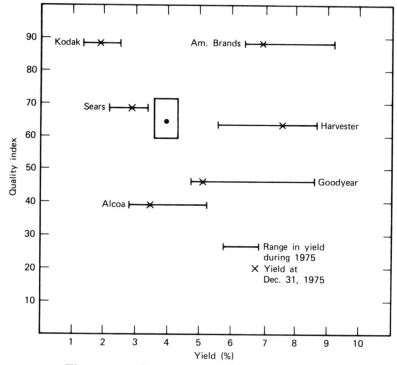

Figure 10-6. Blending six issues of varying quality.

decision-making, not to replace him. Thus, the quality-managed system provides signals to the manager but leaves the final judgment to him.

The theory underlying the quality-managed system, as spelled out in the first four chapters, is derived from the proven and time-tested concepts of MBO and of quality measurement. Most major businesses rely on MBO systems, as do a number of nonbusiness activities. Quality measurement is thoroughly established in the commercial world and has been in wide use for at least half a century. Logic strongly suggests that the MBO concept can be used as effectively in the management of assets as it is in the management of people.

The extensive and voluntary use of quality measurements in commercial enterprises indicates that these measurements strengthen business where employed. If they didn't, the business managers would dispense with them. It seems incongruous that financial assets lack quality measurements since they must support the businesses that do use them.

The easy way to end a book on investing is with an assurance that the wisdom distilled therein will produce untold wealth. These books and assurances are now so numerous that they no longer produce wealth even for the authors.

While there is no guarantee that it will generate great wealth, the quality-management investing system can be relied upon to produce predictable results and peace of mind for the investor. It does not preclude the bonanza that we all would like to see, but, if applied consistently, it will virtually preclude loss.

As has been demonstrated in the earlier chapters, the system can be useful for small amounts, as little as $5000, as well as large funds. The quality/yield objectives are meaningful even to the nonprofessional investor or beneficiary; and, most importantly, the probability that they can be achieved is great enough that they can be both promised and delivered.

To an investor or beneficiary, peace of mind comes with an increase in the cash available to him and an understanding of his status while his money is at risk. The management system and accounting system described herein meet these requirements.

It is not to be expected that the quality-managed investment concept will move quickly from theory to general practice without extensive testing. This can readily be done without committing actual money, simply by managing a "paper" portfolio. Such a course is strongly recommended for the nonprofessional investor so that he can enter into an active investment program with the confidence that comes from knowing his own abilities. The quality-managed system provides that confidence.

APPENDIX A

Calculating the Quality Index and Yield

The vital data required to operate the portfolio management system described in this book are the quality index and the yield. These should be calculated at frequent intervals to determine the status of the portfolio relative to the assigned objectives. Further, it is advisable to make hypothetical calculations in order to determine in advance the impact on the quality/yield correlation of proposed transactions.

Before the advent of computers and electronic calculators, the burden of making these computations would have made use of this management system awkward and laborious. This is no longer the case, and the information in Appendix A provides various methods for programming these calculations.

The essence of the program is shown in the worksheet in Table A.1. In brief, this program is made up of the following steps:

1. Multiply the number of shares (column 1) by the market price (column 2) and enter the result in column 5.
2. Multiply the quality index (column 3) by the product derived in step 1 and store in column 6.
3. Multiply the number of shares (column 1) by the dividend per share (column 4) and enter the result in column 7.
4. Repeat for all of the portfolio companies.
5. Aggregate columns 5, 6, and 7.
6. Divide the sum (or aggregate) of column 6 (quality-weighted market value) by the sum of column 5 (market value) and multiply by 100 to produce the portfolio quality index.

TABLE A.1 CALCULATING PORTFOLIO QUALITY AND YIELD

Company	Code	(1) Share	(2) Market Price	(3) Quality Index	(4) Dividend per Share	(5) 1 × 2	(6) 3 × 5	(7) 1 × 4
TOTALS								

Sum of (6) divided by sum of (5) × 100 = portfolio quality
Sum of (7) divided by sum of (5) × 100 = portfolio yield

7. Divide the sum of column 7 (dividends) by the sum of column 5 (market value) and multiply by 100 to produce the portfolio yield.

These calculations are always the same, no matter what type of equipment is used to do computations.

Using a calculator that does not have a memory requires use of the program shown above with all of the results being entered on the worksheet.

Using a calculator that has a single memory, alleviates the need to write down the results for columns 5, 6, and 7 for the individual companies. They can instead be stored in the memory while being computed and only the column totals need be recorded. Using these totals allows the data for individual companies being considered for purchase or sale to be added or subtracted to provide the hypothetical quality-yield data.

Using a calculator that has a single memory alleviates the need stored while the calculations are being made, and only the portfolio index and yield need be recorded by hand. It is nonetheless advisable to record the totals for each of the results columns (5, 6, and 7) for use in hypothetical transactions. A program for the Rockwell 82R printing calculator is shown in Table A.2 to illustrate the use of two-memory equipment.

TABLE A.2   ROCKWELL 82R PROGRAM

Enter	Comment	Sample
M 1	Open Memory 1	
DS 2	Set for two decimal number	
100	No. of shares, Item 1	
×	Multiply	100 ×
25	Market price, Item 1	
M =	Multiplies and stores, Item 1	2500.00 + 1
+	(Repeat for all items)	
150	No. of shares, Item 2	
×	Multiply	150 ×
30	Market price, Item 2	
M =	Multiplies and stores, Item 2	4500.00 + 1
+		
	Repeat until all market values are stored; then:	
MS	Record Memory 1 Total	7000.00 1

Enter	Comment	Sample
	Shift to Memory 2	
2500	Market value, Item 1	
×	Multiply	2500 ×
84	Benchmark index, Item 1	84 =
M =	Multiplies and stores, Item 1	210000.00 1
+	(Repeat for all items)	
4500	Market value, Item 2	4500 ×
×	Multiply	
78	Benchmark index, Item 2	78 =
M =		351000.00
+		
	Repeat until all items are stored, then:	
MS	Record Memory 2 Total	561000.00 11
÷	To divide Memory 2 total	
	Shift to Memory 1	
MS	To enter Memory 1 total	7000.00 1
T	Completes calculation	7000.00 = 80.14
×	Convert to index	80.14 ×
100		
T		8014
	Shift to Memory 2	
MT	Clear Memory 2	
100	No. of shares Item 1	
×	Multiply	100 ×
.65	Divide, Item 1	
M =	Multiplies and stores, Item 1	65
+	(Repeat for all items)	
MS	Record Memory 2 total	65 11
÷	To divide Memory 2 total	
	Shift to Memory 1	
MS	Enter Memory 1 total	7000.00 1
T	Completes calculation	7000.00 = 0.01
×	Convert to index	0.01 ×
100		
T		1.00

A programmable calculator eliminates the need for a worksheet altogether. A program is included for the Rockwell 930 programmable calculator (see Table A.3) which asks the operator to enter the number of shares, market price, quality index, and dividend. The calculator then produces the quality index and yield. The registers used with this program are listed on p. 149.

TABLE A.3   ROCKWELL 930 PROGRAM

Addr	Instr	Val		Addr	Instr	Val
000	L A			027	C S	
001		8		028	P	
002		1		029	S T	
003	C A			030	L A	
004	L A			031		1
005		1		032		1
006		5		033		5
007	L S			034	C S	
008	L S			035	P	
009	D S			036	S T	
010		0		037	L A	
011	S E			038		1
012		9		039		2
013		1		040		7
014	M			041	C S	
	+			042	P	
015	0			043	S T	
016	x			044	L A	
017		1		045		1
018		0		046		3
019	y			047		9
	x			048	C S	
020		1		049	P	
021		0		050	S T	
022	=			051	L A	
023	P			052		1
024	L S			053		4
025	L S			054	S E	
026		3		055		1

056.........		9	
057.........		0	
058.........	→ M		
059.........		0	
060.........		0	
061.........	← M		
062.........	I N		
063.........		x	
064.........	S E		
065.........		+	
066.........	← M		
067.........	I N		
068.........	=	+	
069.........		x	
070.........	S E		
071.........		+	
072.........	← M		
073.........	I N		
074.........	S E		
075.........		2	
076.........	=	+	
077.........	S E		
078.........		3	
079.........	← M		
080.........		9	
081.........		0	
082.........		x	
083.........	S E		
084.........		+	
085.........	← M		
086.........	I N		
087.........	=	+	
088.........	← M		
089.........		0	
090.........		6	
091.........	J		

092.........		+	
093.........	L A		
094.........		1	
095.........		6	
096.........	J		
097.........	L A		
098.........		1	
099.........		5	
100.........	L A		
101.........		8	
102.........		3	
103.........	P		
104.........	→ M		
105.........		9	
106.........		0	
107.........	J		
108.........	L A		
109.........		1	
110.........		1	
111.........	L A		
112.........		8	
113.........		5	
114.........	P		
115.........	→ M		
116.........		9	
117.........		5	
118.........	D S		
119.........		0	
120.........		+	
121.........	T		
122.........	→ M		
123.........		9	
124.........		1	
125.........	D S		
126.........		3	
127.........	← M		

128........		9
129........		5
130........	+	
131........	← M	
132........		9
133........		1
134........	−	
135........	T	
136........	÷	
137........	D E	
138........		8
139........	D S	
140........		3
141........	=	
142........	→ M	
143........	+	
144........		9
145........		1
146........	J	
147........	L A	
148........		1
149........		2
150........	L A	
151........		8
152........		7
153........	P	
154........	→ M	
155........		9
156........		2
157........	J	
158........	L A	
159........		1
160........		3
161........	L A	
162........		8
163........		9
164........	P	
165........	→ M	
166........		9
167........		3
168........	J	
169........	L A	
170........		1
171........		4
172........	L A	
173........		9
174........		0
175........	L S	
176........	L S	
177........		1
178........		0
179........	C S	
180........	P	
181........	← M	
182........		0
183........		2
184........	÷	
185........	← M	
186........		0
187........		1
188........	D S	
189........		0
190........	x	
191........		1
192........		0
193........		0
194........	=	
195........	P	
196........	← M	
197........		0
198........		6
199........	J	

TABLE A.3 (*Continued*)

200		+		236	L A	
201	L A			237		1
202		9		238		7
203		1		239	L S	
204	L S			240	L S	
205	L S			241	S T	
206	S T			242	L A	
207	L A			243		8
208		9		244		2
209		1		245	S E	
210	L S			246		9
211	L S			247		*
212		1		248	← M	
213		1		249		0
214	C S			250		1
215	P			251	→ M	
216	← M			252		0
217		0		253		4
218		3		254	← M	
219		÷		255		0
220	← M			256		2
221		0		257	→ M	
222		1		258		0
223		x		259		5
224		1		260	← M	
225		0		261		0
226		0		262		3
227	D S			263	→ M	
228		1		264		0
229		=		265		6
230	P			266		0
231	← M			267	→ M	
232		0		268		0
233		6		269		1
234	J			270	→ M	
235		+		271		0

No.			No.		
272		2	298		0
273	→ M		299		6
274		0	300	→ M	
275		3	301	+	
276	J		302		0
277	L A		303		3
278		1	304	→ S	
279		5	305		9
280	L A		306		0
281		1	307	L A	
282		6	308		1
283	← M		309		7
284		0	310		0
285		4	311	→ M	
286	→ M		312		0
287	+		313		1
288		0	314	→ M	
289		1	315		0
290	← M		316		2
291		0	317	→ M	
292		5	318		0
293	→ M		319		3
294	+		320	J	
295		0	321	L A	
296		2	322		1
297	← M		323		5

- 1 SF Main program
- 2 SF Optional issues to add or omit
- 3 SF Number of shares
- 5 SF Market price in eighths ($24.4 = 24\frac{1}{2}$)
- 7 SF Quality
- 9 SF Dividend
- 10 SF Show quality index on option
- 11 SF Show yield on option

After the program has been entered manually once, the machine can record it on a magnetic card for subsequent use.

The quality and dividend data can also be stored on magnetic cards and the program modified to eliminate manual entry of these items. The capacity is adequate for storing an approved list of 50 issues, but each company has to be identified by a numeric code.

Selected Benchmark Index Numbers

In order to assist the reader in operating the investment management system described here, we are including a list of representative Benchmark Index Numbers. These can be used to compute the quality component of the quality-yield correlation. The other essential data, market price and dividend, can be most easily obtained from the stock tables in the daily newspaper.

The numbers listed in Table B.1 are in eight categories, beginning with Benchmark Index Numbers in the range 20–29 and moving successively higher to 90–99. There are 30 stocks listed in each category, only a small portion of the total but adequate for learning, testing, and demonstrating the system.

The index numbers are based on 1975 data and may no longer be current. Accordingly, they should be verified before they are used for investment purposes. The selection has emphasized large companies, which are more likely to be recognized by nonprofessional investors. The inclusion or exclusion of any company has no significance regarding its investment suitability.

TABLE B.1   REPRESENTATIVE BENCHMARK INDEX NUMBERS

20–29 Range

Air Products & Chemical	23	Frantz Mfg. Co.	29
Allied Supermarkets	29	General Binding	28
American Greetings	28	Giddings & Lewis Inc.	20
Ariz.-Colo. Land & Cattle	28	H. J. Heinz Co.	29
Asamerica Oil	20	Interstate United	29
Automated Bldg. Comp.	21	Leeds & Northrup	25
Bangor Punta	28	Mallinkrodt Inc.	27
Bates Mfg.	27	Motorola	29
Beckman Instruments	26	Parker Pen	29
Berkey Photo	23	Skelly Oil	28
Braniff International	27	Tracor	20
Capitol Food Inds.	28	Tyco Labs	24
Carson Pirie Scott	25	UAL Inc.	24
DeKalb Ag. Research	22	Wadsworth Publg.	24
Eason Oil Inc.	28	Zayre	21

30–39 Range

Allied Stores	33	Evans Products	39
Aluminum Co. of America	39	Fairchild Camera	35
Am. Hosp. Supply	38	First National Stores	32
Bausch & Lomb	39	Goodyear Tire	34
Brinks Inc.	38	Green Giant	39
Burroughs	31	Hewlett Packard	35
Chemetron	37	Int'l. Mins. & Chems.	37
Cleveland Trust Co.	36	National Airlines	39
Congoleum Corp.	34	National Tea	39
Curtiss Wright	38	Pet Inc.	32
Dictaphone	34	Polaroid	34
R. R. Donnelly & Sons	39	Rohm & Haas	37
Emery Industries	31	Stone Container	39
Ennis Bus. Forms	36	Texas Instruments	34
Esmark	35	Western Publishing	38

40–49 Range

Anchor Hocking	47	Firestone Tire	43
Avery Products	42	Fisher Foods	43
Becton Dickinson	44	Flintkote	45
Bethlehem Steel	46	Globe-Union	49
Boeing	48	Hart Schaffner Marx	47
Borg Warner	48	Honeywell Inc.	42
Cannon Mills	46	Koppers Inc.	46
Cities Service	49	Macy R. H.	42
Continental Airlines	47	Owens Corning	48
Dart Industries	45	Pennzoil	49
Del Monte	46	Reichhold Chemical	43
Denny's	48	Scovill Mfg.	41
Easco	44	Standard Oil Ohio	48
Emhart	43	Texas Industries	49
Faberge	46	Victor Comptometer	48

50–59 Range

Aetna Life & Cas.	53	Marshall Field & Co.	59
Am. Broadcasting	55	Monsanto	58
Amsted Industries	59	Outboard Marine	54
Atlantic Richfield	54	Reliable Stores	54
Bendix	54	St. Regis Paper	55
Chicago Bridge & Iron	56	Scott Foresman	50
Cummins Engine	53	Standard Oil Indiana	57
Delta Air Lines	57	Tampa Electric	59
F M C	53	Texas Gas Trans.	55
General Dynamics	57	Transamerica	58
Goodrich	56	United Technologies	58
Great A & P	58	U.S. Steel	50
Illinois Tool Works	55	Wells Fargo	53
Johns Manville	58	Westinghouse	59
Kennecott Copper	59	Woolworth	50

TABLE B.1 *(Continued)*

60–69 Range

Abbott Labs.	66	Inland Steel	66
American Express	68	Int. Harvester	63
Annheuser Busch	61	Jewel Companies	61
Ariz. Pub. Service	68	Johnson & Johnson	60
Beatrice Foods	63	Manufacturers Hanover	66
Chase Manhattan	68	Mobil Oil	68
Chrysler	62	Pac. Gas & Elec.	69
Colgate Palmolive	67	Quaker Oats	69
Continental Can	66	Scott Paper	67
Eaton	62	Sears Roebuck	68
Federated Dept. Stores	65	Stauffer Chem.	67
Florida Power & Light	68	Union Oil	64
Georgia Pacific	64	United Brands	63
W. R. Grace	65	Walgreen	68
Houston Nat. Gas	61	Weyerhaeuser	66

70–79 Range

Allied Chemical	72	I T T	75
Am. Tel. & Tel.	73	Marathon Oil	73
Bankers Trust	79	Marine Midland Bks.	71
Borden	74	May Department Stores	71
Caterpillar	78	McGraw Edison	78
Clark Equip.	72	J. P. Morgan	76
Columbia Gas System	76	Nalco Chemical	79
DeLuxe Check	78	Noxell Corp.	75
Dow Chemical	75	J. C. Penney	73
General Foods	71	Peoples Gas	79
Gerber Products	73	Pfizer	77
Gulf Oil	74	R C A	76
Houston Ltg.	71	Revlon	77
IU International	74	Union Carbide	77
I B M	78	Xerox	78

80–89 Range

American Cyanamid	80	Miles Labs.	87
Archer Daniels Midland	81	Otis Elevator	83
Central Telephone	80	Pepsico	81
Champion Spark Plug	87	Proctor & Gamble	82
Du Pont	88	Russell Stover	84
Eastman Kodak	87	SevenUp	88
Emerson Electric	81	Standard Brands	85
Exxon	86	Sterling Drug	89
Ford Motor	87	Suburban Propane	82
General Electric	87	Tenneco	84
General Telephone & Elec.	81	Texaco	84
Gross Telecasting	85	U.S. Gypsum	86
Hershey Foods	88	Upjohn	85
Liggett & Myers	88	Warner Lambert	88
Lilly Eli	86	Wrigley	87

90–99 Range

Avon Products	95	Maytag	94
Block H & R	94	McGraw Hill	91
Bristol Myers	92	Merck & Co.	93
C B S	90	Nabisco	93
Chesebrough Ponds	92	Prentice Hall	90
Coca Cola	93	Republic Steel	97
Dun & Bradstreet	94	Royal Crown	91
Emery Air Freight	96	Schering Plough	92
General Mills	91	Searle	96
General Motors	94	Smithkline	94
Gillette	94	Square D	94
Heublein	97	Squibb	91
Kellogg	92	T R W	94
Libby Owens Ford	92	United Telecommun.	94
Marion Labs.	94	Zenith Radio	93

Index

.ndex